Clients From Hell

A collection of anonymously-contributed client horror stories from designers

Channel V Books
New York

Channel V Books
New York

Copyright © 2011 by Channel V Books

INTERIOR DESIGN: Brandon Velestuk

Published in the United States by Channel V Books,
a division of Channel V Media, New York, NY
www.ChannelVBooks.com

Channel V Books and its logo are trademarks of Channel V Media

ISBN 978-0-9824739-3-1

Library of Congress Control Number: 2010932185

Library of Congress subject headings:
Work--Humor
Interpersonal relations--Humor
Work--Anecdotes

PRINTED IN THE UNITED STATES OF AMERICA

10 9 8 7 6 5 4 3 2 1

First Edition

"ABANDON ALL HOPE, YE WHO ENTER HERE."

Sure, they're not our words, but they might as well be. In truth we owe a certain amount of credit to Dante Alighieri, whose 14th-century *Inferno* provided the inspiration for understanding the 21st-century sleazeballs we've come to know—and loath—as Clients From Hell.

In Dante's Hell, sinners inhabit concentric circles of increasing malfeasance, with those guilty of the least egregious sins—Limbo and Lust—suffering at the edges and those who have committed the most terrible sins—Fraud and Betrayal, for example—consigned to the inner layers. While we make no such distinctions—in our minds all Clients From Hell are equally deserving of our contempt—there is some truth to Dante's characterization. For that reason, we find that the lesser sin of Limbo is incredibly well represented in the coming pages—we can (almost) feel sorry for these sinners since it's (almost) possible to believe they know not what they do. And we should probably take some comfort in the fact that stories about the more dire offenses are far less common. But alas, we will not rest until we've exposed all sinners, regardless of their crimes, for what they truly are: Clients From Hell.

We pity the poor designer who endures any level of grief at the hands of a Client from Hell. All the more reason to hope that Dante's punishments hold true when Hell calls back its demon spawn, and that these worst of the breed will suffer a level of pain proportionate to that which they've caused.

So, without further ado, prepare to be transported across the River Acheron…

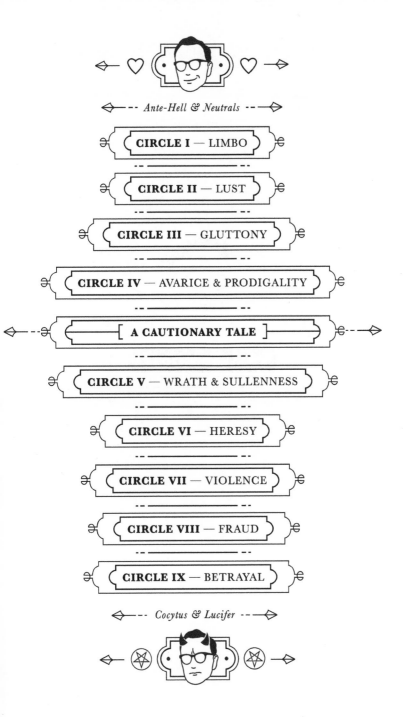

Ante-Hell & Neutrals

CIRCLE I — LIMBO

CIRCLE II — LUST

CIRCLE III — GLUTTONY

CIRCLE IV — AVARICE & PRODIGALITY

[A CAUTIONARY TALE]

CIRCLE V — WRATH & SULLENNESS

CIRCLE VI — HERESY

CIRCLE VII — VIOLENCE

CIRCLE VIII — FRAUD

CIRCLE IX — BETRAYAL

Cocytus & Lucifer

INTRODUCTION

Most people who work in the design industry can agree that the clients we serve fall into one of two categories: good and terrible. True, this was but a pessimistic hunch when we launched the Clients From Hell blog in January 2010, but ever since, we've seen overwhelming confirmation of this hastily-formed hypothesis. As I sit here writing this, we have well over a thousand submissions awaiting us, each detailing some surely-macabre client horror story.

If our contributors are anything like us, they probably had no idea just how common their situations were until they found our community of similarly disillusioned designers and creatives. Communal empathy is the backbone of the Clients From Hell blog, and though we launched hoping that others might commiserate with stories at least as bad as ours, we quickly discovered that there's always room to be outdone.

It all started on a Friday afternoon after a series of particularly difficult calls with three different clients. After hanging up with the last of the bunch, we were forced to consider an uncomfortable possibility: what if the reason we were consistently running into the same issues with different clients was that we were the difficult ones? After all, client management isn't exactly what we signed up for.

Feeling the sting of insecurity, we launched Clients From Hell in a desperate attempt to validate ourselves. Within a few months, we'd received an overwhelming number of dispatches from designers around the world and a monthly readership of over a million people.

Our craft is a strange hybrid of art and technology, both of which are highly mystified and often intangible. After all, you can't pick up and handle a piece of web design—it's completely abstract. We've never considered a client's lack of technical knowledge a sign of subpar intelligence; it's a lack of common sense and an abundance of self-righteousness that really irks us. We also recognize that while we all think of ourselves as artists first and foremost, the day that we started accepting money for our work was the day that we entered the customer service industry—a place that has been historically plagued by outrageous requests and malevolent behavior.

We hope that this book will give you some painfully honest insight into the reality of working with far too many clients—enough, at least, to provoke some deep-rooted sense of community and empathy for your fellow designer soldiers. While I'd like to say that the stories featured in this book are rarities, we've found that they're all too commonplace. The stories we've included belie any false conception that bad client relationships are simply the result of a little miscommunication; in fact, as you'll read in many of these stories, any semblance of rational communication is often hard to come by. It's a rough world out there for a designer trying to make it the way he or she knows best. Now, on to the horror stories...

— *Anonymous Editor*

CIRCLE I — LIMBO

Hellish clients have an uncanny way of getting stuck in the nebulous space between should and shouldn't, decision and indecision, strategy and spontaneity... And the list of polar purgatories goes on. They hold up projects forever without approving them, flood your inbox with a barrage of last-minute requests, and make a million irrelevant changes, all in an effort to compensate for their incompetence—at your expense.

CLIENTS FROM HELL

The 14 Worst Words a Designer Will Ever Hear
"I'm not sure what I want, but I'll know it when I see it."

Alert the Internets
"Make sure you tell the Googles of the world that the site will be launching soon so it places high in their results."

Translator, please?
I had a client review a design, and all the text areas contained 'Lorem Ipsum.'

> CLIENT: It looks good, but we don't understand it.
>
> ME: What don't you understand?
>
> CLIENT: The text. What language is that anyway?
>
> ME: It doesn't mean anything; it's just placer copy to help you visualize where the text will go. Just focus on the design for now, not the content.
>
> CLIENT: [*after a day or two*]: Could you please type the text from our brochure in there? We can't review the site in a foreign language.

Gender Discrimination Against Mother Nature
"We were wondering if you could possibly use snowflakes that look a little bit more masculine."

"Instead of edits or comments, I've just drawn sad faces in places where I don't like the copy."

Normal Wear and Tear
"Can you re-upload the photos on my site? I think they're fading from so many people clicking on them."

Totally Hip

While working on a project targeting tweens, our clients nixed all of our ideas (even though the focus group testing numbers were off the charts), and started throwing in their own ideas. The clients were all in their late 40's, and their concepts were pretty much cringe-worthy. When our boss politely mentioned to the clients that creative teams fresh out of school probably had a better grasp on youth market trends and interests, the client snapped back, "I think I have a grasp on what *youngsters* find *groovy*."

"You can't make that movie poster design black and white — people will think the movie is in black and white."

No Shoes, No Socks, No Service

Upon presenting a design to a client, he removed his shoes, plopped his stocking'd feet up on the desk and said, "As you can see, you didn't knock my socks off."

My nonprofit client is really pushing for this tagline:

"Learning should be for everyone. *Everyone*."

I would like to nominate it for the Overemphasis of the Year award. *Overemphasis of the Year award.*

Don't Let the Terrorists Win

I put an icon that looked like an atom on a business application. Upon sharing it with the CEO who hired me to design it, I received some constructive feedback:

> "I'm worried about that icon. You know, because of Iran. It will make people think about their nuclear program."

CLIENT: I love the website, but I can't look at it on my computer. Can you put it on a DVD, so I can go through it on my telly?
ME: Not really. A website isn't a movie and it wouldn't work on a DVD. You need to view it in a browser on your computer.
CLIENT: What's a browser?
ME: It's a program you use to view websites. Do you use Windows? You probably click the big blue 'e' when you look at the web, right? That's Internet Explorer, and it's your browser.
CLIENT: Oh, right, I thought that was the Internet?
ME: Well, yes, sort of… Listen, I'm not sure what the problem is. Why can't you view the site in your browser?
CLIENT: My computer is switched off.

Pixel-nomics

CLIENT: How big is the graphical header?
ME: 700 pixels wide.
CLIENT: It's too small. Can we make it a half pixel bigger?
[*I roll my eyes and then email him the exact same image.*]
ME: Here you go.
CLIENT: Perfect!

Later in the project, he asked if we could reuse pixels to save money.

"Right next to this 'GET STARTED TODAY' button, can we add a sentence that reads 'CLICK HERE NOW' with an arrow pointing to the button? I'm just worried people won't know where to click."

"We can't make the type black or white because Apple owns both of those colors."

The client looks at the storyboard and says to the bearded copywriter, "Seems to work okay, but I'm not sure anyone in my commercial should have a beard. Normal people simply don't have beards."

CLIENT: Can you get rid of the gradient on the screen?
ME: That's a glare. Tilt up the monitor a little bit and it will go away.

Cursed With the "yme?" Chromosome
In the review stage for a clothing retail site where primary navigation has been stripped down to 'Women', 'Men' and 'Magazine':

CLIENT: Can we move the 'Magazine' link over to the right, away from the other navigation? It might confuse people who don't know if they are a woman, a man or a magazine.

"If I press the 'home' button, where will it take me?"

"Let's go with a kid-oriented look. Bright colors, fun elements and I already picked out a font I thought we could use. Do you have Comic Sans?"

"So I shared your rough design concepts with my wife's child-birthing class to get their feedback."

"Your display ad has been sitting on my desk all day, and I tell you, it keeps catching my eye. When I'm working on something else, I keep glancing over at it — I can't help it. Can we fix that?"

Designer Moonlights as Psychic
"You're the designer; why do you need information from me?"

"Are you nuts? How are you going to map out an entire website plan on a piece of paper? You're going to need a piece of paper that's bigger than this entire building! That would have to be the biggest piece of paper ever made!"

"I can't access the Internet from this computer; I haven't downloaded Google yet."

CLIENT: The password for the CMS doesn't work.
ME: What password did you use?
CLIENT: [Password]
ME: Oh, I see. That's because the password is wrong.
CLIENT: Okay, thanks.
[*Two minutes later...*]
CLIENT: 'Wrong' doesn't work either.

"Can you put page numbers on the two-sided postcard? I'm not sure people will know how to get to the other side."

"We don't want anything interactive. We tried the Internet once—it didn't do anything."

"Can you make it more Kanye?"

"There's too much white. Let's fill it up. I want to make sure I get my money's worth."

"Can you please rotate the logo 360 degrees?"

"I'm not going to tell you anything because I don't want to limit your creativity."

> **CLIENT:** Our site has been hacked—there are little orange boxes all over it!
> **ME:** Yes, those are RSS feeds. You'll see them on all major sites.
> **CLIENT:** Well, they look like hacking to me.

The Moron Constellation

> **CLIENT:** I'm having a problem with my password.
> **ME:** How so?
> **CLIENT:** When I type it in, it turns into stars.

"I've made the corrections in red, but I don't actually want you to put the text in red."

"I was thinking that rather than silence we could just have, you know, the sound of nothing."

"I've printed it out, but the animated GIF isn't moving."

What time does your website open?
"We need our website to work during regular business hours—from 9 am to 5 pm, Monday through Friday."

"We like neutral colors, like lime green and purple."

Logo Sommelier

"The logo color is 'wine.' Not as dark as a full-bodied Merlot, more like a cheap Côtes du Rhône."

CLIENT: Well, how big is your computer?
ME: My, uh… How big?
CLIENT: Yeah. How big? Big enough to handle a big sign?
ME: Well, it's a newer MacBook Pro, so I shouldn't have any trouble.
CLIENT: No, like how many inches?
ME: It has a 17-inch screen.
CLIENT: Well, that won't work. It's a big sign. We need something that's thirty- or forty-inches wide.

CLIENT: That font right there! It's clean, yet edgy. There's NO WAY I've seen that before; I would remember! What is it?
ME: Arial.

A Sign of What's to Come

The first point in the client's brief: "The website will be available online."

CLIENT [*after changing a source in the CMS*]: I changed the file name to 'logo-blue.png' and it didn't turn blue; it turned into a small box with a red 'X' in it. Have you broken it?

CLIENT: Hmm, could you make it bigger?
ME: That's what she said.
CLIENT: You're out.

</Déjà vu>

"The site's broken. When I'm on the homepage and I click the 'back' button, it takes me to another site."

CLIENT: The site looks great, but I need you to do another one, too.
ME: Umm...okay...what for?
CLIENT: You know —you made the website on a Mac so you need to make another one on a PC for people who don't use fancy computers like you!

"Your sales rep showed us a commercial we really liked. It was shot in front of a green screen, though—I'm wondering if you have any other colors to choose from."

"Thanks for the PDF, but can you resend it at 100% instead of 147%?"

"Can you add a menu to the beginning of this VHS tape? You know, like a DVD, so we can skip forward."

A Font from the Wrong Side of the Tracks

"I hate this new font. Use the first one I showed you. This one makes the site look cheap instead of elegant."

Note: The "cheap" font was Georgia. The "elegant" font was Georgia Italic.

Subliminal Message

"When users login, I want them to see an animation of a bank safe opening. That way, users will know they can trust us."

> **CLIENT:** I love what you've come up with here, but I think we need some blue-skies thinking.
> **ME:** Can you explain what you mean?
> **CLIENT:** You know, thinking outside of the box, pushing the envelope. I just don't think we're both singing from the same hymn on this one.
> **ME:** Can you explain without using business jargon?
> **CLIENT:** Maybe we can touch base later on this?

Devil's in the Details

> **CLIENT:** The ad with the big digits is fine, but I don't like the '9.'
> **ME:** Why?
> **CLIENT:** It looks like an upside-down '6.'

"Can you change the color of the headline? Black text scares old people."

My client, the lolcat.
A sentence from a client's email:

"Plz moves this link closer to teh paragraph and teh headings close to teh start of the text"

---

5 words I hate...and hear daily:
"Just have fun with it."

The Company Idiot

A client called complaining that she couldn't access the company website. When I arrived to troubleshoot, I found that she'd typed the following into the browser: "the company website."

"I'm so glad I found someone who could make the Internet."

"I really like the CD cover you made, but my guitar looks out of tune."

Can't Argue With That Logic

ME: The logo on your website doesn't need to be so large. It's not like it's going on the side of a truck going 90 mph on the highway.

CLIENT: Yeah, but it *is* going on the information super highway.

CLIENT: Capitalize the numbers in our phone number so they stand out more.

ME: That's not possible.

CLIENT: Yes it is—just hold down the *SHIFT* key and type our phone number!

Friends for the Friendless

A client recently hired me to create a social networking site...

CLIENT: I like Facebook, but I don't like having to approve friends.

ME: What do you mean?

CLIENT: It takes too long for someone to approve me. On my site, I want all friend requests to be approved automatically.

ME: What if the user doesn't know or want the individual to be their friend?

CLIENT: Who doesn't like having lots of friends?

"When I scroll down the page, the header and logo disappear."

Alternative energy source?

At a trendy restaurant in NYC, with our prospective client and her "marketing consultant," our prospect downed two drinks in rapid fashion...

CLIENT: Our product is going to become ubiquitous in the marketplace. We need millions of customers.

US: That's great, how do you plan to achieve this?

MARKETING CONSULTANT: We're going to use the power of the web.

CLIENT: Yes, we want you to help us harness the power of the web to get our product out there.

US: Can you be more specific? There are many tactics...

CLIENT: How can I be more specific? The power of the web is it.

CLIENT: Please make the date of the event Thursday, June 18th.

ME: Don't you mean, "Friday, June 18th"?

CLIENT: No, you see, we have the Friday confirmed but we really want to hold the event on Thursday. So, let's make the typo intentional, that way it works for whatever date we end up with.

ME: Your FTP password is literally one of the five most commonly-used passwords in the world.

CLIENT: I guess great minds think alike!

CLIENT: I want you to put the search box at the bottom of my website. I'm tired of all those websites with search boxes at the top — they're way too "in your face." I want my visitors to really want to search.

ME: Umm...you want them to search for the search box?

CLIENT: Exactly.

Marketing people in Germany like to use the English language to give products or events an appearance of internationalism and modernity—even if their own language skills are somewhat lacking.

One of our German clients asked me to create promotional material for a camping trip where participants would meditate, focus on their inner strength, and so on. The good news was that she'd already come up with the perfect English name for the outing: "concentration camp."

CLIENT: When this gets printed, what colors get mixed together?
ME: Well, anything that gets printed is basically some combination of black, yellow, cyan and magenta ink, or toner…
CLIENT: That's not going to work. I'm printing these for boys, not girls, and magenta is a girl's color. Take the magenta out of your printer and replace it with red. Red is much manlier.

CLIENT: I'd like for a hockey puck to fly around the screen as the information on our homepage loads. The cursor will be in the shape of a hockey stick, so visitors will have to whack the puck before we let them in the site.
ME: I'm going to do everything in my power to talk you out of doing that.

"No, that's not right. That color is too chocolate; it needs to be the color of baby poop."

Recommended Daily Allowance of Excitement

"Can we change the font of 'Saturated Fat' and 'Sodium' to something more exciting? We need people to have a positive feeling about them. And while you're at it, let's put the percentages in little stars so they think it's a good thing that they are so high."

"I know what will make this easier... Holograms!"

CLIENT: So, we are looking for a "partnership" with Google.
ME: Okay, how and what exactly do you want?
CLIENT: Since we don't have a website yet and our budget is only $500, we want to buy the website google.com and redirect all the hits to some custom landing page that people can rent space on!
ME: Err... I don't think Google will just let you have their domain name...
CLIENT: Can you at least give them a call? I know a guy who works there—just ask for him and it will be fine, I'm sure!
ME: So, you want me to call Google and offer them $500 for their domain name?
CLIENT: Yes, start with $100, so we have some wiggle room to negotiate if they want more.
ME: Right.

"Please call me if you don't receive this email."

"We've identified our target audiences. They're 50% female and 42% male."

"The typography does not please us. Too much 'Tim Burton', not enough pirates. "

CLIENT: Because this is the first time we've met, I want to be completely upfront and honest with you. About five years ago I was in a mental institution, but then I found Jesus and he showed me a vision. That vision is what I want to discuss with you today.

ME: Okay. How can I help you?

CLIENT: I want you to design some business cards for my company. I fix air conditioners.

CIRCLE II — LUST

Sure, it's normal to covet your neighbor's ~~wife~~ cool gadgets and gear, but acting on one's every covetous desire and impulse can transform a standard case of envy into flat-out creepiness. This client is never satisfied with your work because he always finds someone who's done something bigger, better and badder, and he's just got to have it. But let's not forget the client who's lusting after more than just things: The client who speaks fluent sexual innuendo. Or the client who sits just a little bit too close. It's bad enough when a Client From Hell is lusting after some*thing*, but when a client starts lusting after some*one*, it's time to sound the alarms.

CLIENTS FROM HELL

I.
Lusting after some*thing*…
(Thinking *inside* the box)

"I really like Apple's logo, so I've taken it and put our name under it."

The Sincerest Form of Flattery

"I knew I liked your work from the moment I saw your logo. Since we need a logo, can we just use yours, but replace your company name with ours?"

Via the contact form on our company website…

Hi,

A friend gave me your business card. I want a business card just like it for my dog-grooming business! And I'd like it if you could put your logo on it in the top left corner. Then, in the top right corner, I'd like you to draw a picture of a dog getting a bath. I want the same pink you used for the background on your business card, but everything else should be black because my business is black and white. In the bottom left corner, please put my name and address, and in the bottom right corner put my phone number and email address. YOU MUST USE BLACK INK!

I think that's it. How much will this cost and how quickly can you get it done? I don't think it should be very expensive because I don't need a new logo if I'm using yours. Can you please send me an estimate ASAP?

CLIENT: Can you make a special "M"—you know, like the one on the McDonald's sign?

[*After I explain…*]

CLIENT: What do you mean it's copyrighted? How can someone copyright the letter "M"?

All PR is Good PR

CLIENT: I'd like to use [cartoon mascot of a large corporation] on my advertisement.

ME: Sorry, but that cartoon's trademarked. You can't use it.

CLIENT: But they haven't used it for 25 years.

ME: It doesn't matter; they still own the rights.

CLIENT: So what? Use it anyway.

ME: No, I'm not getting sued by a huge multinational corporation.

CLIENT: Why not? Just think of all the great publicity we'd get.

Baby Steps

I asked a client if her business had a logo to use in its ad, and she said she would email it over. When I opened the attachment, I saw that it was the Gerber logo. The text in the email read, "This is our logo. We're going to need you to cut off that 'Gerber' part and put our company name there."

CLIENT: I already know what I want for my logo. My store's initials are N and Y, and I'm a Yankees fan, so I'd like for you to use the logo the Yankees have on their hats.

ME: Well, I can't just swipe the Yankees logo. They own that.

CLIENT: Oh, well could we use it if you modified it a bit?

ME: How would you like it modified?

CLIENT: I don't know, maybe make it red?

CLIENT: We need our ad to look exactly like the one from the Seattle store.

[*The Seattle store was owned separately, and its ad was designed by a different agency.*]

ME: Well, I can't just steal their ad.

CLIENT: Yes, you can. I have permission from on high. It's okay.

ME: Okay, permission from whom?

CLIENT: My boss.

ME: But your boss doesn't hold the copyright to the ad.

CLIENT: He doesn't need to; he said it's okay.

ME: […]

CLIENTS FROM HELL

II.
Lusting after some*one*…
(Thinking *about* the box)

"Let's put a border around it. And can the border throb a little? I want it to throb."

Inspirational Imagery

> **CLIENT:** I have the photos that inspired the project on my phone. I can show you what I'm talking about.
>
> *[Client holds the phone toward me and scrolls through the photos with his finger.]*
>
> **CLIENT:** See, these colors. Here's another one…
>
> *[Client scrolls a little too enthusiastically, and lands on a photo of his smiling face next to a giant erect penis.]*
>
> **CLIENT:** Oh! Ha! Not that one.
>
> *Meeting continues uncomfortably for another 20 minutes.*

Fetish Confit

While developing an affiliate website for one of our mobile network clients, my boss came over to review our progress.

> **BOSS:** I think we need to have some sort of avatar on the homepage—something that welcomes users to the site.
>
> **ME:** No problem. Did you have anything particular in mind?
>
> **BOSS:** Well, since sex sells, I'd like to feature a slim, sexy female cartoon character holding a mobile phone.
>
> *[I proceed to create a sexy avatar.]*
>
> **ME:** I've finished the avatar. Is this what you were after?
>
> **BOSS:** That's nice, but not exactly.
>
> *[Here, my boss conducts a Google search and pulls up an image of a small, chubby, animated duck holding a mobile phone.]*
>
> **ME:** I thought you wanted a sexy woman?
>
> **BOSS:** I do.
>
> **ME:** Apparently you're into some kinkier shit than I am.

Hair Sample

My client asked me to go to a meeting with him and his boss. When I got into the passenger seat of his car, I immediately noticed part of a girl's weave on the floor...

ME: What's that hair on your floor?

CLIENT: Oh that's just pet hair. Some dog or something must have left it behind.

ME [*Slightly confused. I know I shouldn't press the matter, but my curiosity trumps my sensibility.*]: This is definitely human hair. I can see the end of the weave.

CLIENT: Oh, well, um, no. I think it's probably just dog hair. Yes, it must be dog hair.

[*Long pause*]

Maybe it's hair. I don't know. It's not like I'm a murderer or anything. Don't go snooping for fingernails or anything like that."

[*Awkward laugh*]

ME: Yeah, I wasn't thinking that...

CLIENT: And I'm not a cross-dresser or anything like that. I'm not gay. Umm, can we not talk about this anymore? I'd like to act like this conversation never happened.

ME: Yeah, that's perfectly fine.

CLIENT: I'm really not gay.

Nothing else is said for the remainder of the 25-minute car ride.

Blowjob Barter

CLIENT [*after giving me the details of his new website*]: How much will that cost?

ME: Well, you've given me a lot of information. I'd like to organize my notes and get back to you with a proper quote.

CLIENT: I'd like to get it going as soon as possible. How's $250?

ME: Uh... That's a little low. I'd feel more comfortable giving you an official quote and then working out a payment plan.

CLIENT: All right, how about this: I'll give you $250 for this project, and then guarantee that you get the next project I'm working on. It's a porn site for this 70-year-old woman. So, that's $250 AND 15% of the profits from that site. Also... I'll blow you.

"Just spray your creative juices all over it!"

Overruled

Our client was a leading home insulation manufacturer. Because the government recommends a minimum of 12 inches of attic insulation, we designed a simple brochure with a perforated ruler that our client could offer to contractors/remodelers, who would, in turn, share it with homeowners. Homeowners could then use it to measure the insulation in their attics.

Not a bad way to get homeowners to think about and buy more insulation from the client, right? Right. Unfortunately, the client ultimately killed the piece because they thought the contractors would just take off the rulers to measure their penises. Clearly, a legitimate concern...

Text from a client at 7 PM on a Sunday night:

"I have to run downtown right now to pick something up. Will you come along to keep me company?"

After Hours

> **CLIENT:** So, what do you have planned for this weekend?
> **ME:** I have no idea. Why, what's up?
> **CLIENT:** Well, do you ever do any escort work?
> **ME:** Uh, no.
> **CLIENT:** I mean, I need to go to a dinner and I'm supposed to bring a date.

In the Name of Productivity

"Next time we meet, you might wear something a little more low-cut. We'll get more done."

"We like the woman in the wheelchair, but we don't want people to think being in a wheelchair makes her less feminine. You need to make her breasts larger."

After telling a client that I couldn't go out on a date with him because I have a policy against mixing work/pleasure (a boldfaced lie, of course)…

"Conflict of interest is the new vested interest."

Not exactly a client story, but…

In response to a job listing my firm posted for a graphic designer, a woman sent in a very unique portfolio. Almost the first dozen pieces were mediocre photo manipulations of her face on other women's bodies—all of whom were posing with A.J. MacLean from the Backstreet Boys. One even featured her head awkwardly pasted on top of a nude woman receiving a back massage from the pop star. She wasn't hired.

A client calls at five of midnight and whispers, "Is it too late?"

"Can you tell me what time you're going to bed tonight? I need to know when I have to stop calling you."

It's Not That I'm Undesirable; It's That You're a Lesbian

My business partner and I (we're both women in our early 30s) had dinner plans with a business prospect. Though we were supposed to meet at 7, he kept emailing to say that his flight had been delayed, but he was coming, so please wait.

By the time he arrived—at 9:30—he was completely wasted, and revealed that—oops!—he'd actually been playing golf all day and that's why he was late (but went out of his way to emphasize that he cut it short because he "had a sense we were hot").

After downing two martinis in quick succession, he began staring at my partner's legs with little attention to anything else. When I suggested that we order food (a little something to absorb the alcohol), he turned belligerently from the legs to me, and growled, "What are you, a lesbian?"

As this charmer had been referred to us by one of our best—and favorite—clients, we felt compelled to stick it out, and over dinner (during which he continued to consume drink after drink), we listened to him rotate among his prowess at business (and the Lotus he was going to buy), why he was going to leave his wife (while leering at my partner's breasts), and how it was that I came to be a lesbian (i.e., cockblock).

The next day, we were surprised to see an email from him land in our inboxes.

Its contents? A suggestion that we meet for dinner again soon…*since he was too drunk to remember our evening.*

"I was looking at your pictures on Facebook and thought, *Wow— there you are in a bikini…*"

Background Check

"Before we start working together, can you please send me a picture of yourself? I only want to work with good-looking people."

When visiting a client to learn more about the company and what they do:

"I thought about having you stay in our basement instead of at a hotel—it would really piss off my wife and I'd love to see the look on her face in the morning."

A client, approximately 55-years-old, came up with an ad campaign idea based on the premise that "[product name] is better than Viagra®." In order to illustrate this, he let me in on the following details (on a long car ride, during which I was his captive and totally uncomfortable audience):

"My equipment is working better than any 30 year old's."
"My tool is perfectly intact; it just needs to be taken out for a spin."
"My machinery is well-oiled and up to date."

Paging Sigmund Freud...

CLIENT: We want our logo to feature one of our industrial steel columns. How about one large tower with two smaller storage tanks along the bottom?
[I draw a long vertical shaft with two round circles at the base...]
ME: Like this?
CLIENT: PERFECT! Let's roll with it.

"It was good to see you today. You know I have a thing for brunettes."

"Wow, your headshot is great. I'm going to print it out and frame it, and tell everyone you're my girlfriend."

I Thought I Saw A Pussycat

A client sent me an email containing a screenshot of what was going wrong on his site. In the middle of adjusting the code I received the following message:

"URGENT: If you ever publish that screenshot, I'll have you blacklisted from the industry and never pay another invoice again!"

Not knowing what he was talking about, I re-examined the screenshot. In the Google toolbar, I noticed that he had searched for "Nicole Scherzinger Naked XXX."

Worst. Game. Of. Charades. Ever.

CLIENT: Can you make it sexier?
ME: I'm not sure I understand what you mean by "sexier"? Do you want a more elegant font or…?
CLIENT: No, I like the font; I just want it to be more, well, sexy. You know…SEXXXXY?!
[Here, the client begins gyrating his hips.]
ME: That's really not helping.

I was hired to do a couple of illustrations for a story about people who are asexual (meaning that they do relationships, but they don't do IT).

I sent my sketches to the art director and received an email back that said, "These look great, but could you possibly add some whimsical-looking dildos?"

Oh, *That* Hair's Breadth
Creepy client is standing behind me at the computer in the studio, "art directing" me over my shoulder.

"Okay, now let's move that text just one pubic hair higher."

Speaking in Tongues

> **ME:** Are you bilingual?
> **CLIENT:** Yes. In fact, I'm cunnilingual.

Title on a job listing:

"TALENTED AND HORNY ILLUSTRATORS"

"You're pretty enough to be a stripper. If this graphic design business thing doesn't pan out, talk to me."

A client who owns a tanning studio has the initials "B.J." and she signs all of her emails "xoxo bj." Aren't hugs and kisses awkward enough?

"If I was ever going to sexually harass anyone, it would definitely be you."

CLIENT: This looks good. I'd like for you to get together with the project manager and the marketing director for a little ménage à trois before the next phase of the project starts.
ME: Excuse me?
CLIENT: Oh, ménage à trois? That's a French phrase. It means "collaboration."

CLIENT: I'm sending you the cover photo now.
ME: Cool.
CLIENT: It's a cute photo, but please be sure to cover up the little boy's penis.

"You can call me anytime. I'm available at night. Late, late at night. So, you'll call me one night?"

"I keep looking at this website, and it just isn't blowing my skirt up."

"Please stop using 'cont.' as an abbreviation for 'continue.' I keep on reading it as 'cunt.' Thanks."

"It's a poo fetish website, but it needs to be classy."

I was in a meeting with a new employee, rehearsing for a product demonstration we were to deliver together. The lights were off and I was standing at the front of the room by the projection screen when I said, "This is the part that really shows off what our application does. This is where we get the client excited about it." The new employee's immediate response was to hoot and holler like a maniac, and pull her shirt over her head to reveal her bra.

I immediately left the room and went across the hall to the first office with a door on it. I walked in and closed the door. Two female coworkers were in the office. I sat down. One of them asked me what was wrong. Before I could explain, the new employee followed me into the office. I asked her to leave. The other coworker again asked what the problem was, to which the offender replied, "Oh, it was no big deal. I just lifted up my shirt… Like this!" She proceeded to do it again, horrifying her audience.

The next day, I went to get advice from another coworker. "Should I talk to her?" "Should I talk to my boss?" "Go right to HR?" Just as we were discussing the options, I look out the window next to his desk. The woman is standing on the street with her shirt pulled up over her head, showing her breasts to a friend on a motorcycle. No bra this time.

CLIENT: Look, forget all of these ideas. I've got a new idea: make a logo that fucks.
ME: A logo that fucks?
CLIENT: Yeah, a logo that fucks everyone who looks at it. Like Microsoft's.
ME: Okay, I'll come up with some sketches…

"I want you to design something that will make people horny when they see it."

CIRCLE III — GLUTTONY

Gluttonous Clients live in a constant state of "more"—a land of "and," "I need" and "how about..." Whereas in the real world more work is synonymous with more money, you'll have no such luck when dealing with a Client From Hell. The only things you'll receive more of are demands, neediness, patronization and insults. Gluttonous Clients laugh in the face of fair compensation.

CLIENTS FROM HELL

The "I'm Going to Get You to Commit to the Project and Then I'm Going to Lowball You" Client

"A thousand dollars is very expensive, you know. We just want a simple website with our current content and a contact form. And don't forget about a user-friendly CMS—we want to add and edit content on our own. And the picture gallery—we want something that's stunning and animated. The header should be animated as well. And our logo seems too old— can you design a new logo for our company? The best price we can offer is $300, and we think that's more than enough."

"The problem with you college students is that you always expect to get paid for the work that you do."

No Questions Asked

"I can't pay for this right now, but I have about a dozen old computers in my garage. I'll tell you what: if you design this for me, I'll give you an hour alone in there with no questions asked."

Gluttony Disguised as Self-Awareness

An email from a random prospect...

Hi,

I need to have a book laid out and designed (front/back covers). I can offer you an insulting $200 Canadian for your time, plus a copy of the printed book upon its completion.

Please let me know how offensive you consider this offer or, conversely, how desperate you are for work of this kind and that you will accept this project unwillingly.

Thanks.

"Can't you just take shittier pictures for a discount?"

It's Just Words and Colors

> **ME:** The total for your new logo, business cards and menu design is $350.
>
> **CLIENT:** Are you kidding me? The reason I chose a student designer was to get something cheap, plus help you expand your portfolio. I could have gone to a professional and paid much less.
>
> **ME:** Um, that's not true. I spent a lot of time dealing with your daughter who insisted on multiple revisions to the logo, and you ended up with a look that everyone is pleased with. This same project might have cost you 10 times the amount I'm charging you. It's a great deal.
>
> **CLIENT:** I highly doubt that. It's just words and colors. Plus, our satisfaction has nothing to do with the amount we pay you. I'll send you a check for what I think is fair.

I received a check for 100 bucks, and he'd written, "Here you go, asshole" on the memo line.

> **CLIENT:** I need to know the exact amount of time it took you—in minutes—and that's what I'll pay you for.
>
> **ME:** I'm sorry, but I told you that I work by the hour. I don't work by the minute.
>
> **CLIENT:** I'll pay you for the minutes it took you, not the hours. How long did it take?
>
> **ME:** 60 minutes.

> **CLIENT:** How about we pay you in free alcohol?
>
> **ME:** Only if I can make your poster out of macaroni noodles.

Photoshop Facelift

CLIENT: Okay, now don't make me look ugly. Oh, and can we make my nose smaller? I hate my nose. And don't give me chubby cheeks. And definitely don't draw the acne at all. Is that cool?

ME: Sure. So, who would you like me to draw instead?

Let's Take a Moment to Reflect Upon Your Ignorance

Our art director had flown from the UK to Florida to take a shot of a beautiful old Ford Mustang. Back in the UK, the account manager says the client is unhappy with all the palm tree fronds.

ACCOUNT MANAGER: Can't we just Photoshop some of them out?

ART DIRECTOR: Well, it's not quite as easy as that, because if you look at the shot, there are reflections of the palm fronds in the car's glistening bodywork. They'll be harder to remove.

ACCOUNT MANAGER [*Slightly flustered; indignant*]: Yes, but if you remove the actual palm fronds, then the reflection of them will disappear, too.

No Bueno

CLIENT: The English version of the site looks good. I was thinking we should make Spanish and Portuguese versions of the site as well since the site will mainly reach a South American audience.

ME: Umm... You told me the site was mainly for an American audience. I could do it, but I don't speak any of the languages. Can you send me the translations?

CLIENT: Oh, that's no big deal. Just copy and paste the English text into Google Translate. Just make sure to check those versions for spelling and grammar errors.

"I really love it but can you change the colors and design?"

Small

"Can you add an infinitesimal amount of red?"
"Can you make the circles a little bit rounder?"
"Can you green it down 10% and make it six-inches wide on the monitor?"
"Can you move that logo up 1/63 of an inch?"

CLIENT: I've got very clear ideas for the logo.
ME: That's great, tell me about them.
CLIENT: Well, I thought it was your job to figure that out. Why don't you send me several concepts, and I'll tell you when you get close?

"We really don't like the web as a medium. Can you please force visitors to print out a copy of every page? We want our site to be more...tangible."

Just a few small changes...
"We need you to change the header font to Comic Sans MS and incorporate the illustration of the soccer goal into it. Oh, we also want a flash header, where the welcome text will fade in alongside a soccer player chasing a ball across the screen. Can this all fall within the same price?"

"I'm thinking I want five or six different logos for my business. That way I can put a different one on my website, business cards, and T-shirts, and really stand out from the competition."

Wizardry and Fireballs: Just Another Day at the Office

ME: Okay, we've made the site live.
CLIENT: Why isn't the site #1 on Google yet?
ME: It just went live five minutes ago.
CLIENT: Optimize the fireball.
ME: I'm sorry? Do you mean the firewall?
CLIENT: I need more hits NOW, so I need you to optimize the fireball. I know what I'm talking about!
ME: We'll get right on it.

The "I Don't Know Why You Always Have to Argue with Me" Client

CLIENT: We need to use WeirdoFont on our website.
ME: That's not possible—it's not a common web font.
CLIENT: Nothing is impossible! It's just a question of time and money.
ME: Well, OK, I'll travel around the world and install the font on all internet-connected computers, if you can get the copyright clearance for the font.
CLIENT: That's more like it! You'll be ready for launch next month, right?

"I want you to make it so people have to give us their email before they can look at the site. If they're gonna look at our stuff, I want to be able to spam them afterwards."

Clear Instructions

"Make sure it's not too edgy, not too flashy, not too detailed, not classical/traditional, not too complex or exciting, but not all over the place, efficient but fun, clean, fresh, modern, upbeat, contemporary, legible, smooth, shapeless, timeless, not outdated, but simple."

CLIENT: Hey, I'm just calling to drive you crazy…
ME: At least you're being honest…

"Just make it more good."

Your World. Not Deliverable.

CLIENT: I have three new images to add to your workload this month.
ME: We have already reached the limit on my retainer for the month, so these will have to be pushed back to next month.
CLIENT: But I still have images left over from the retainer from September!
ME: I'm not AT&T; I don't offer rollover images.

CLIENT: Can you send us another copy of our logo?
ME: I've already sent it over to you three times this week.
CLIENT: Well, I've used all those now.

The "I Need Several Options to React to" Client

"I don't know what I want until I know what the final product looks like. So, I would like you to create five fully-functional websites, so I can make an informed decision and then pay you for one of them."

Romper Room RFP

We received a child's coloring page, featuring a cat playing an electric guitar, along with the following note:

"Please color this page so we can get a sense of your creativity. This will help us decide whether or not to hire you."

Actual email from a band:

K so we want album work done, just a cover fpr a cd and of course a logo on it we are releasing an E.P that is we are pying about $2000 for and we want it to be superb. we want it to be really super cool and epic. detailed and precise our budget.. we will discuss it. we want an angelic demon hybrid, holding a very hot and innocent, dead, sort of cut up but not mutilated young woman in the air as if the demon had just conquered her. in the back round we want to have a mas-sacred old feudal village with a church on top of a hill long aban-doned and some mutilated people scattered around the village. and a dark purple sky with clouds. the ground should be swampy and have boney hands of corpses popping out as if trying to reach the mistress. our logo should be readable, the most insanely cool and epic think that you can think of and dimensional with perspective. you can play with it until it looks good to you. totaly metal. make it fucking rad as hell, seriously we are paying a lot for this thing to get cut so please fucking rip up the screen with this.. give us some ideas about cost. we are going to pay practicaly as soon as we here from you...

"I will pay you when my website becomes popular like Facebook. For now, you can just work on it."

"The Board is not willing to pay for a website during tough times. We feel that there are many unemployed web designers who would be happy to volunteer their talent."

"Can you include an intro animation that turns the screen into a mirror so that visitors can see themselves? We really want to push the metaphor."

CIRCLE IV — AVARICE & PRODIGALITY

Collectors and hoarders. Under-users and wasters. Typical clients and demon spawn sent to this earth to make your life a living hell. Just a few of the characters you'll face when working with Clients From Hell whose sins are Avarice and Prodigality. Characterized by an excessive desire for wealth or gain (Avarice) or excessive wastefulness (Prodigality), these clients are marked by their outlandish demands or expectations, not to mention an extreme lack of awareness of the amount of work it will take to meet those demands (assuming it's even possible).

CLIENTS FROM HELL

"Please erase all other Google search results showing our competitors' websites immediately. If you cannot do this, we'll be forced to take legal action against you."

CLIENT: Can I have the illustrations that we commissioned?
ME: No problem, I'll burn you a disk.
CLIENT: No, I want the actual illustrations.
ME: But they were created digitally. They don't exist other than on a computer. If you want to frame them, I can get them printed out on some nice paper for you.
CLIENT: No, I want the originals.
ME: But you're not understanding: the originals were created on a computer. They don't exist on paper.
CLIENT: So why did they cost so much?
ME: Sorry, I don't know how to answer that.

"The video looks great! Now upload it to YouTube and make it go viral."

"I want a MySpace-type site for kids, like ages 1 through 5."

In response to the Twitter background we designed for a client...

CLIENT: I like it except that the main Twitter panel in the middle covers some of the copy on the side.

ME: Yes, you've stumbled upon one of the fun quirks of Twitter. Since you're not willing to budge on the sidebar content and images, users with smaller screens are going to experience this when they go to your page. Basically, it's because Twitter opts to keep the main content area a fixed width (so no matter what screen you're on, that element will always be the same width), and the background image is forced to compensate. If you look at other people's custom backgrounds on that same screen, you'll likely notice that some of theirs do the same thing—well, that is, if they have the same amount of copy as you. But if you look at them on a larger screen, they won't. I think that's the long way of saying that it's difficult to avoid this without either getting rid of some of your text/graphics, or without making the graphics really small and the text illegible, which would obviously pose a whole new array of issues.

CLIENT: I figured this was about screens, but I'm confident you can make it work.

"The unicorns don't look realistic enough."

CLIENT: We really love the design, but can you make our website less cutting edge? Our clients aren't really that good at using the Internet and won't use all of the bells-and-whistles.

ME: What 'bells-and-whistles', specifically, are you referring to?

CLIENT: We don't need the login area. None of our customers will use that.

ME: Okay, well it's an e-commerce store so I'm not quite sure how you're going to get paid without being able to identify the client.

CLIENT: Well, you're the designer and you've done a great job so far, so I'm sure you can figure something out. Look at Google—you don't have to log in to their site and they're making tons of money!

"I don't want to use the word 'improved' in the copy because it will make our new product look better than our old product."

I was working on a brand identity for a client and we were discussing paper for their stationery. I made some recommendations and the client called to ask me to email him a sample of the paper so he could feel it. After two minutes of arguing that I cannot email a physical sample, the client said, "Okay, fine. If you can't email it, then just fax it to me."

Why didn't I think of that?

"We want a site that's like Facebook, YouTube, Flickr!, and Twitter all rolled into one. Oh, and it will need to have an e-commerce solution."

Visionary or seeing things?

"I already know what I want for the logo: a house, with a face. And it's on wheels with an exhaust pipe coming out of the back, which is shooting out smoke in the shape of dollar signs."

Negative Charge

"Can you send over that logo in electron form, at the highest granularity you have?"

"I want to make a website that only people in Nashville can see."

"We can't use a photo of peanut-butter sandwiches—my daughter is allergic to peanut butter."

Armed and Dangerous

A marketing manager from a convention center contacted me about retouching some event images taken during a speaking series. He wanted to repurpose them for use in an upcoming newsletter about the past season's notable speakers and events. In particular, some of the images were of a semi-famous climber who lost his arm during one of his climbs and is now doing motivational speaking engagements.

When going over the job specifications, he eventually revealed to me that the item that needed retouching was the climber's arm—they wanted to add it into the picture. Somewhat shocked at the request, I asked him to explain more specifically what he needed, just in case I'd misunderstood.

"I don't see how I can be any clearer: just make a copy of his right arm, reverse it, and stick it on his left shoulder. We don't want to alienate our attendees by putting a depressing picture in the newsletter."

"That photograph looks too unrealistic—can you add more reality?"

CLIENT: We'd like the background color to be a bit whiter.
ME: The background color is already white, #ffffff.
CLIENT: Is there anything whiter than that?

CLIENT: I would like you to incorporate my cats into the logo.
ME: OK, I can add a cat illustration to it.
CLIENT: No, I don't want the cats illustrated.
ME: Should I set up a session with a professional photographer then?
CLIENT: You can't do that—they both died ten years ago. I'll send over some snapshots of them. Just make them glow, sort of angel-like.

"I want the design to look like five people standing outside a theater, having a conversation after a movie, waiting to be picked up by a car…dipped in gold."

"Can you make it so when people open their browsers, my website automatically pops up?"

"Well, that's very nice so far, but, well, have you seen *Matrix Reloaded*?"

Unkempt

"The grass in your rendering looks too clean-cut and cared for. The maintenance crew doesn't want to guarantee that it will be kept up that well. Can you make it more overgrown and brown with some dead patches?"

Crimes Against Common Sense

CLIENT: Can you un-blur the background on this photo?
ME: Un-blur?
CLIENT: Yeah, I want the whole image to be super sharp. I don't particularly care for that whole deep field thing you keep telling me about.
ME: You mean depth of field?
CLIENT: Yeah, whatever. Just un-blur it.
ME: That's impossible.
CLIENT: I've seen it done on *CSI*.

"If you erase the top of the building in Photoshop, the sky will be behind it, won't it?"

"We need to see this person's face [*points to a person in the photo with his back to the camera*]. You need to turn the person around 180 degrees."

"I want it so that whenever someone visits our website, an icon with a picture of a dog is automatically installed on their desktop. The dog should then walk around the screen."

Money-Back Guarantee

In a meeting with a client, who asked us to sign an NDA before coming in...

CLIENT: I need to put together a big online dating site. We're gonna need ways for people who don't have digital photos to scan in their bio pictures, and we're gonna need a big database where we can store all of this. I'll also have you guys manage everything going forward.

ME: About how many customers are you expecting?

CLIENT: Oh, just hundreds of thousands. It's gonna be HUGE.

ME: OK, based on your description, we're looking at (very large amount of time) at (very large amount of money) to get everything done for you. We're going to have to ask for a deposit of one-half so we can start work.

CLIENT: Well, I can't pay that. I'll make the money after it starts, and then pay you.

ME: Sorry, but we'll have to decline.

CLIENT: But you don't UNDERSTAND. This is GUARANTEED to make money!

"Most of our photos feature white people, but we need to show more diversity. We don't have the budget for another photo shoot, but I'm sure you can just change them to various races. I mean, that's what a graphic designer does, right?"

"All these drawings of dinosaurs… Why can't we just use photos?"

"Above all, when you redesign the website, I don't want any HTML in it. I'm tired of dealing with all the hassles of HTML."

"Of course I want it today! If I wanted it tomorrow, I'd order it tomorrow!"

Silent Partner

> CLIENT: I have a great idea, and I'd like to bring you on board as a partner.
> ME: Go on…
> CLIENT: It's great. I want to recreate Google, but make it better.
> ME: How?
> CLIENT: Well that's where your expertise comes in.

"Can you take this photo of me and my baby and rotate the baby so you can see more of his face?"

Kettle. Black.

"Can you make our website track users' webcams? I want to make sure that nobody on our site is a creepy-stalker type."

CLIENT: We want a script that disables users' ability to right click so that people, by which we mean *pedophiles*, can't save pictures from our gallery of kids.

ME: But the gallery has an 'email me this picture' form.

CLIENT: Yes, but that's for parents.

CLIENT: I need you to design me an internal company newsletter.

ME: Sure, I'll need the logo, brand guidelines, any relevant graphics and text.

CLIENT: You're not licensed to use those.

"Make the site have the contact information hidden between the lines, like subliminally. I want our clients to be smart enough to figure it out, and when they do I want them to remember the information forever."

CLIENT: For the homepage we'd like a photo of San Francisco—lots of tall buildings and it has to include the Golden Gate Bridge.

ME: Sure, I can do that, but your offices aren't in San Francisco.

CLIENT: No, but we want people to think they are. It creates trust.

"I need a website. The information on the website is top secret, so I need it up only during business hours, as to avoid hackers and competition from getting a hold of the information. I'd also prefer we hosted it on a Mac."

Disarming

"The woman in this photo is perfect, but she needs to be disabled. Can you Photoshop her so she only has one arm?"

Dim Bulb

"We were thinking that if you just Photoshopped the lamp off of the table, you'd be able to see the kids playing behind it a lot more clearly."

Superdouche

"We'd like to illustrate the power of our new product in our presentation, so we're thinking we'd like a man in a business suit flying through the air with a cape… But we want the cape to be a screenshot of our website."

CLIENT: We love our new building and we thought it would be great to take pictures of it in all four seasons, from the exact same angle.

ME: That sounds cool.

CLIENT: Great! What are the chances of having those ready for our convention next month?

CLIENT: Can you remove the man's hat?

ME: Yes, what kind of hair would you like him to have?

CLIENT: You'll find out when you take off the hat.

The Truth Hurts

CLIENT: I Googled my name and there is some nasty stuff about me on the Internet. There is this guy blogging about what an idiot I am. I want you to remove that blog and block the Internet if they write that shit about me.

US: We can't do that.

CLIENT: Well, get someone else to do it then. I want every nasty thing about me removed from the Internet today, and make sure nobody can write bad things about me. I want you to control the Internet.

US: We can't control it, and neither can you.

CLIENT: Right, if you can't do it, I'll find someone who can.

Webmaster of the Universe

The client calls around 9 o'clock on a Saturday evening. When I don't answer, he calls back eight more times in rapid-fire succession. I email him from my phone, figuring this was an urgent problem.

> **ME:** I'm not available at the moment as it's Saturday. What's the problem?
>
> **CLIENT:** Please check our website—it's not working AGAIN.

[I go to the website and it's down. Looking into the matter, I find that the domain name has expired. The domain name was registered by his organization, so my company has absolutely no control over it.]

> **ME:** We did some research that indicates that the registration may have run out. Your organization registered and managed the domain name, so I can't help with this since we have no involvement in managing the domain name.
>
> **CLIENT:** I am reading your email in disbelief. You are the webmaster—how can there be an aspect of our website that you don't control?

> **CLIENT:** I've got the perfect image for my album cover. My girlfriend is sitting on her bed wearing red lingerie with photos of me all over the place. The photos are all on fire, and she's screaming as she tears up a photo of me and dumps it into a marble bowl.
>
> **ME:** Okay, can you send me that image, or does it need to be shot?
>
> **CLIENT:** No, you have to make it in Photoshop 'cause we broke up.

> **CLIENT:** I want a proposal for this great idea I have.
>
> **ME:** What's the idea?
>
> **CLIENT:** I can't tell you because it's confidential.
>
> **ME:** How can we provide you a quote when we have no details?
>
> **CLIENT:** You can sign an agreement saying that you won't work on a similar project for two years.
>
> **ME:** How can we sign an agreement for an idea we have no information on?
>
> **CLIENT:** You will make millions...

The client has sent a picture taken on his camera phone and wants to use it in an A4 brochure...

ME: Hello, I'm phoning regarding the image you sent earlier. It's way too small; it's only 640 x 480 pixels. Ideally we could use something 10 times that size. Also, it's out of focus. We essentially just can't use it; it would look pretty terrible if we enlarged it.

CLIENT: Ah, I see. Can't you do anything with it? Can't you work your usual magic on this?

ME: I'm afraid not. It's simply not of high enough quality for an A4 magazine ad. If we could get a high-resolution photo taken by a professional photographer, we'd be in good shape.

CLIENT: Can't you just wave your magic wand and make it better?

ME: I'm not Harry Potter.

CLIENT: I'm very disappointed in you.

Blue Ocean Strategy

CLIENT: We would like our commercial to run on BBC1.

ME: The BBC doesn't run ads.

CLIENT: Well, you are supposed to be the big media man; you need to get our commercial on BBC1!

ME: No one can run commercials on the BBC, they simply don't air them.

CLIENT: So, we can totally own the BBC if there are no other advertisers! This is going to be great.

ME: No, it's not.

"Can you make the 'S' into a dollar sign?"

Basic Geometry

"I want them to be rectangles, but I want them to have the feel of triangles."

"Lime green instead of regular. As ninja-turtle bright as possible."

After the client, a Catholic church, received a mock-up of a brochure...

"The brochure looks great, but we'd prefer to use a photograph of Jesus instead of a painting."

ME: I'll create a login box on your website. Once someone registers and logs in, the website will recognize who the user is and provide relevant content.

CLIENT: That sounds great. However, instead of a login box, I'd like to use biometrics to identify the user.

ME: I'm not sure what you mean.

CLIENT: When someone visits the website, I want them to be able to put their hand on the monitor. The monitor will then scan their hand to confirm who they are. I think that would be a lot more engaging. How much extra would that functionality cost?

ME: Several hundreds of millions of dollars.

CLIENT: Why are you being a wiseass? Can you do it or not?

ME: No, sorry. That's a little too advanced.

CLIENT: Fine. I'll try another web designer.

Final Cut ~~Pro~~ Dumbass

CLIENT: You know about Final Cut Pro, right?

ME: Yes.

CLIENT: I hear there is a button that makes the video go into focus.

ME: What do you mean 'into focus'?

CLIENT: Well, I shot video but it's all out of focus and I hear there's a button that will fix this for me.

ME: I don't think that's possible.

CLIENT: I thought you said you knew Final Cut Pro.

Crimes Against Common Sense

CLIENT: Can you un-blur the background on this photo?

ME: Un-blur?

CLIENT: Yeah, I want the whole image to be super sharp. I don't particularly care for that whole deep field thing you keep telling me about.

ME: You mean depth of field?

CLIENT: Yeah, whatever. Just un-blur it.

ME: That's impossible.

CLIENT: I've seen it done on *CSI*.

A CAUTIONARY TALE

We here at Clients From Hell thought we had long passed the point when anything could shock us. We receive stories every day that make us gasp in horror, so it's only the rarest occasion that we read something so utterly appalling—so sickening—that we can't think of an appropriate impersonal, humorously detached reaction. Instead, we want desperately to put our editorial hand on the author's shoulder and say, "It's gonna be okay."

When we received "A Cautionary Tale," it really hit home. Maybe because it was a longer story that allowed us to connect with the author. Maybe because it featured a whole cast of characters—the sympathetic hero, the loathsome villain, and a few in between—or maybe simply because we were reminded that the stories we hear aren't always just funny or cringe-inducing, but the result of the trials of real lives and real people. Whatever the reason, the story reminded us of a sobering fact: behind so many of our stories, there's a frustrated individual who's been truly worn down emotionally and mentally by a client.

When we first posted this story, our readers flooded us with an outpouring of sympathy for the designer. We even received messages from people wanting to offer him free legal advice. For a few weeks, the Clients From Hell community came together in a mass-loathing for the hellish client and unadulterated sympathy for his victim.

Unfortunately, we can't tell you much beyond what the designer reveals about his or herself in "A Cautionary Tale" since this has been our only point of contact. Even so, we find we can't share this story often enough. If the clients in this book truly are from hell, the megalomaniac at work here may be Satan himself.

— *Anonymous Editor*

I'm sure none of you are strangers to being asked to do favors for friends and family. I'm here to tell you that while there's nothing wrong with doing a favor for someone you love now and then, always draw up a contract and terms of service, no matter how small the project. I don't care if you're doing it for free—make them sign a contract. In this case, I assume complete responsibility for everything that happened because I mistakenly worked from trust. I should also warn you that this reads more like a bad romance than anything else, but, hey, whatever you choose to call it, I wouldn't wish the following circumstances on anyone.

Background: I'm a 22-year-old university student with aspirations to practice rural medicine. I'm also a freelance web/print designer. It's my sole source of income, and it's what I do to put myself through school. I don't have much of a social life because I balance a full-time university schedule with twenty to thirty hours a week of volunteer and paid design work. I wouldn't change a thing. I'm happiest a-codin' and designin', and I count myself pretty lucky to be able to make a living from my hobby while I'm working towards my doc dreams. I've always been nerdy and creative, so I got into computers and art at a fairly young age. I knew I liked designing and I spent a lot of time playing with Python to pick up on basic programming in middle school. In high school, I designed posters and crappy Geocities websites for nearly every extra-curricular club around. So when I was 15, I was really excited when my dad asked me if I'd be interested in doing some design work for a good business acquaintance of his, whom I'll refer to from now on as CFH (for Client From Hell—what else?). The job involved developing some simple layouts and promotional materials for an industry-specific print career guide. Armed with Publisher and Photoshop, I got to work.

The pay seemed pretty damn great for someone my age, and the idea of getting paid to do something I loved from home was attractive compared to the notion of finding a summer retail job, an experience that had bored me out of my mind the previous year. I did the job, CFH was happy with my work, and I continued working on small projects for him every now and then, past graduating high school and entering university. In early 2009, I received a scholarship to study abroad for a semester. When CFH heard, he gave me his heartfelt congratulations, attended a goodbye party my parents had for me, and he even gave me a generous monetary gift for my travel expenses. He become a very supportive family friend at this time, and was often the only non-South Asian face at family gatherings. I was really grateful for his support and thought the world of him.

When I returned six months later, CFH let me know that the website I had designed for him had been voted into the global top ten in its field and that he would be branching out to cover a greater range of clientele. I knew that it was making him boatloads of money, and I was happy to have been involved in a project that had achieved such status. He asked me if I'd be interested in taking a lead role in helping out with the company's growth. I agreed enthusiastically and got to work. Fast forward to September, when I started as CFH's primary web designer. The work was substantial and took up much more of my time than previous projects had, but I completed it on time and he was thrilled with it.

Prior to starting, I had let CFH know that I'd be changing our previously casual business relationship, and that I'd be invoicing him all official-like from now on since I was going to be using my work as my primary source of employment and needed to keep good records for tax purposes.

My first invoice must have taken him by surprise. By this time, CFH had started outsourcing all his back-end development work to India because it was cheaper than hiring Canadian-based developers (yes, this story takes place in Canada—no need to worry that Clients From Hell are an American-only breed), and he had clearly decided that web work was "cheaper" and "easier to do" than print design work. But don't think I billed him for anything more than the barest minimum: I was asking for what was essentially cents above minimum wage per hour of work, and not even including the many hours I spent on development, consultation, edits, etc. Since I was a little insecure in my legitimacy as a designer due to my lack of formal education in the subject, I was more than willing to make concessions and undersell myself. I now know it was silly of me to so undervalue myself—especially as my current clients continue to hire me based on my diverse skills, along with the highly creative and efficient nature of my print and web work. Nevertheless, I decided to give CFH a very steep discount because we hadn't pre-negotiated the terms (even though he was aware of how much time each project was taking me).

He took his sweet time responding to my invoice but finally, and begrudgingly, he paid up. But the story doesn't end there. Before long my interactions with CFH would go from annoying to downright ridiculous.

Despite my better judgment, I continued to work with CFH, who was becoming increasingly imposing. His phone calls to me became longer and less related to work, and often bordered on uncomfortable. He started demanding additional work be done "immediately," and when I'd ask about payment, he'd get irritable and say it was "all about the money" with me, and that he'd pay me as soon as I sent him an invoice via snail mail. Every time I mailed out an invoice, however, he'd complain about some charge and insist that I send him an updated invoice with this or that detail changed.

This continued. I didn't see a cent. I was even paying for stock photos and fonts out of pocket yet wasn't being reimbursed as promised. Keep in mind that I was in a particularly delicate position given that CFH was my father's good friend, and as I now regret, my pride got in the way of actually saying anything to my father at the time. In any case, I assumed I was then suffering through the CFH's most egregious behavior. How could things get any worse?

But they did. So, in January, I put my foot down. I told CFH I'd no longer be working for him as he had become unbearably imposing and had unreasonable expectations of me. Primarily, I was concerned because I hadn't seen a cent—other than that one grudgingly-paid original invoice—for the vast majority of work I'd done since September. CFH responded by telling me that I was a rip-off and that he'd found a "professional design agency" that was better equipped to meet his needs. I wished him the best despite the fact that I was disappointed at having let go of my biggest client. I tried not to think about the many hours of work I wouldn't be seeing a cent for anymore. At the same time, I was relieved that I wouldn't have to put up with his borderline psychotic behavior or compromise the quality of my work anymore to meet his increasingly ass-backwards demands. (White text on beige? Really?!) Two days after our "break up," I received a phone call from CFH. He apologized profusely right off the bat, said that he'd pay me for all of the work I had done, and that he needed me to come back. He told me that he was extremely unhappy with the quality of and the speed at which his new designers were completing work. He begged me to come back, saying that this time he'd be more considerate of my time and reasonable in his expectations of me. I hesitated but agreed— with the stipulation that before I would work on anything, he had to agree to my advance estimate for each job. Since my prices were "too steep" for him and he didn't want to contend with the fact that I could only work in the evenings due to my class schedule, we worked out a system wherein I would design the main graphical elements and primary pages, and his "professional design agency" would use these elements to develop subsidiary pages for the backend.

He agreed and I got to work.

[*As a sidenote, I should mention that his "professional design agency" wasn't nearly as accommodating as I was and pulled out when they realized the extent of the work (in relation to what CFH was willing to pay) and CFH's unreasonably demanding nature. But I digress...*]

Little did I realize that my new agreement with CFH would become a one-way ticket to hell, with him reigning as chief Satanic commander. Despite our new agreement, it didn't take CFH long to resort to his old tricks—and to add some new ones to his repertoire. His behavior began bordering on unbelievable: he'd call me at 11:30 pm asking to have something by 7 the next morning. He'd whine when I said it wasn't possible. He'd have me sit on the phone for hours while directing me to this stock photo or that website to "get inspiration" (his nice way of saying "steal this work").

At the time I was under a lot of stress because I was simultaneously suffering a flare-up in an existing neurological condition that was landing me in the emergency room almost every week. I mentioned to CFH at one point that I was scheduled for an MRI in a couple of months, and he suggested that I pay out-of-pocket to get it done privately to avoid the wait. Apparently my condition was inconveniencing him, and he didn't like to think that all my waking moments might not be his for weeks and months to come. Since a private MRI has to be done out-of-province and runs upwards of $1,500, I explained that this was not an option for me. Thanks to a recent astronomical increase in tuition costs and my student aid having been cut substantially, I was hardly in a position to take on such an overwhelming—and unnecessary—expense. Unsurprisingly, he didn't "get it," and told to bug my parents for the money or "something." For the record, I'm completely financially independent and had no intention of harassing my parents for money I'm perfectly capable of making myself. My lifestyle is hardly so lavish that it requires a lot of dough either: I'm a herbivore, don't go out much, share an apartment with two other people and ride a bicycle or take public transit everywhere. I use open-source software and recycle hardware whenever possible. Textbooks (which I generally buy secondhand) and tuition are my major expenses. While my living expenses might not have been overwhelming, I was still constantly mindful of them and of living within my means. I wasn't sure why this was so difficult for CFH to comprehend. Surely, he must understand, having himself been a student forty years ago?

April brought the final straw. I hadn't seen a cent since September despite many (false) assurances that "the check is in the mail!" and ever more outward confirmations that CFH was doing very well financially. Yes, he was reaping the rewards of my work and had more new business than he could handle. At one point, his many outstanding invoices still unpaid, he even had the nerve to call me to share his excitement about his new "keyless" car, which, he readily volunteered, had cost "about as much as a house." Myriad other offenses followed (and please tell me if I'm being a bit too sensitive here): Rape jokes? Check. Racist remarks about his Indian developers DESPITE the fact that I'm South Asian, too (but "not like one of them," according to him)? Check. Pictures of and forwarded emails from women he was sleeping with? Check. Pervasive questions about my sexuality and personal life? Check!

And so I quit. I fucking quit.

I sent a politely-worded email explaining that I would not be working for him anymore. I don't believe in leaving people in the dark about my decisions or how their behavior might have shaped those decisions, so I explained, very clearly, exactly how his actions drove me to end our relationship.

CFH responded by saying that he hadn't "bothered to read my email" but that "as a professional, [he] anticipated that [I] would provide [my] assistance in bringing the new resources up to speed..." Regarding my invoice, his exact words were: "It shall, of course, be paid, in full, upon receipt" (all those commas, must be, compensating, for, something). I had no problem with this and made the remaining incomplete files available in their raw form on my server, along with a detailed explanation of what the new designer(s) would need to know. I'm not a vengeful person, so when the new designer got in touch with me, I was quick to direct him and to get him up to speed. I just wanted to get paid and to get CFH out of my life already. At the very least, things seemed like they were ending on a slightly more positive note.

A few days later I got a call from my father. CFH had taken him out for drinks and then persuaded him to call me to "tell me" to come back to work for him. CFH had explained to my unsuspecting father that I was upset about my pay (Who knew zero dollars was pay?), but that this was all only the result of a misunderstanding since he had "forgotten" that I was now a grown-up with financial responsibilities, and not that same fifteen year old who was ecstatic about getting some spending money from his hobby. He lamented to my dad that I had left him hanging despite having given me a pretty decent deal. The only thing CFH could conclude, he told my father, was that my "mental health issues" and "greed" had gotten in the way of my professionalism.

At first I simply told my father I would not be working for CFH again. Clearly, this wasn't about the money for me anymore, and I knew that CFH was once again without a designer. (Who else would put up with what I had?) But when my dad expressed his disappointment that I would not work for his friend, I finally let go of my pride and gave him a (heavily censored) full account of CFH's behavior.

On top of all this, CFH still owed me for the work I'd already completed. I actually let myself believe for a moment that I might, at long last, get paid—after all, hadn't he told my father he intended to pay me?

I put the invoice in the mail for the fourth time. Of course, I knew better than to set my expectations too high, and sure enough, on

May 11, I received the following message: "Let me be quite clear about things. Unless you immediately finish the projects you started for [Company Name], we shall not pay your invoice. Enough is enough!"

Over 300 hours logged since September, and I will never see a cent. CFH continues to use my work and profit from it. I have no legal recourse because (1) CFH happens to be a retired lawyer, and (2) I never drew up a physical contract because of the sporadic nature of the work and our long-standing business relationship. I have no one to blame but myself.

The best part? I have to defer my next semester at university in order to work because I couldn't come up with my minimum tuition payment this year. Since the job I had put every free moment into didn't pay me, I had to use my existing fund for things like rent, medication and food.

CFH is well aware of this.

Sucks, but I'm not one to dwell in the past after having recognized my own mistakes. I'm also far too grateful for things like a roof over my head to feel sorry for myself.

But I've learned my lesson. Since then, I have had no problem putting it into practice with my current clients. Though they are primarily charitable organizations and student groups with very limited funding, they respect my time and sign contracts without complaint, agreeing to my terms and putting down a 50% deposit before I do any work. These clients believe in my right to make a living wage from my work and understand that in exchange for my holding up my end of the bargain, they have an obligation as well.

In closing, don't make the same mistakes I did with CFH. I don't care if you're making invites for your neighbor's son's friend's girlfriend's baby shower: always draw up a physical contract, regardless of whether the work is for-pay or not. It's a sad fact, but there is no guarantee of sanctity in a long-standing relationship regardless of how long you have had your client. There are people out there whose only motivation is to make as much money as possible while taking credit for your work and screwing you over in the process. A contract gives you some legal backing and at the very least ensures that both parties understand the terms of service. Deposits are great too because they ensure that both parties are invested in the project to some extent. These are lessons better learned earlier than later.

And finally, to CFH?

I trust Karma.

CIRCLE V — WRATH & SULLENNESS

The most common of the Client From Hell archetypes is the client who suffers from an overall shitty attitude. This client's modus operandi is to be angry, bitter, passive aggressive or just plain psychotic—things that make it hard to wake up in the morning and nearly impossible to fall asleep at night. In the most severe cases, you might even begin to think it's your fault—that the client is actually reacting to you. After all, people can't be this innately unpleasant, can they?

CLIENTS FROM HELL

Some [Don't] Like It Rough

ME: Okay, so here are some rough concepts I've worked up. Once you've…

CLIENT [*interrupting*]: What the hell am I looking at? These look like scribbles my five year old could do.

ME: Oh, they're just roughs I put together to get the concept figured out. Once we agree on the concept, I'll begin work on the actual piece.

CLIENT: How am I supposed to decide which illustration I like if I can't see the finished product? Finish them and then I'll decide which one to use.

ME: Well, I can certainly do that, but just so you're aware, I'll have to charge you for bringing each of these concepts to a finish.

CLIENT: Who do you think you are to make demands?! I'm the client; I get to make the demands! It's not like this is a real job anyway. All you're doing is drawing.

Decoded

My boss charges into my office furiously, two days after the company site goes live.

BOSS: Carl just showed me that people can right-click our site and view all of our code.

ME: Well, yes, that's how web browsers work.

BOSS: Take the whole thing down, now! I'll be damned if I'm going to give our competitors all our goddamn code!

ME: I used dummy text to display the layout—it means nothing.

CLIENT: Well, it needs to be in English so delete it all ASAP. Actually, I've seen this text in Apple's word processor, are you copying Apple?

ME: It's Lorem Ipsum, standard dummy text used in mockups.

CLIENT: You're bullshitting me. Take it off so I don't get sued.

ME: Okay.

CLIENT: Hello, I have an idea for a website. It will be a site about corrupt lawyers and politicians. America is READY to know the truth! We will put a lot of links on it and millions will come to the site. After that we are going to SELL IT for $10,000,000! And my webmaster will get 20%!

ME: It will take a lot of time and work for your website to attract that many people.

CLIENT: YOU DONT WANT TO MAKE $2,000,000?! THEN I DON'T WANT TO FUCKING TALK TO YOU!

CLIENT: I want the site to be metallic and cool—like, "blow your head off" cool. Like the Transformers…

ME: This is for a wedding photography business, right?

CLIENT: So, what? Optimus Prime can't shoot a fucking picture?

Disclaimer

I received a call from a prospective client yesterday. I knew it was going to be a long conversation when the first words out of her mouth were, "I'm not going to lie, I'm bipolar, but I'm taking medication so I should be able to get through this phone call."

The Sky Is Falling

After developing a custom e-commerce site, we received an irate phone call from the client on the day of launch…

CLIENT: We've been hacked! How could you let this happen?

ME: Why do you think you've been hacked?

CLIENT: There's an order right here and no payment!

ME: Who's the customer?

CLIENT: It says, "Mr Testy Tester, 1 Test Street, Testville." It's clearly a hoax order!

ME: You do realize we've been testing the site?

CLIENT: Oh, I see…

Redneck Plumbing Company

Three hours after sending a proof to a client who requested a "pretty ad that reflects the South":

"Git rid of that gay moonlit night and Spanish moss hangin' from them trees. Put a rebel flag on it and we'll be straight."

CLIENT: I hate the logo. I really, really hate the logo. I can't bear to look at it. It makes me sick just to see it. I want you to design another one!

ME: Umm, why? You approved it a few months ago.

CLIENT: Yes, but you knew I didn't like it then. You need to change it.

ME: You approved it. You had your business cards printed.

CLIENT: Yes. I hate them, too!

ME: If you want a new logo, we'll be happy to help, but we would have to charge you for it.

CLIENT [*almost screaming*]: What? Why the fuck should I pay you for something that I hate! You pressurized [sic] me into approving it. I can change my mind if I want to. It's my prerogative as a customer to change my mind. And I hate the website, too.

ME: You had the opportunity to change your mind during the design process, but you didn't. You approved everything. And what's wrong with the website?

CLIENT: I fucking hate it!

ME: But it's exactly what you asked for.

CLIENT: I know it is, but I've changed my mind. I can do that. And I'm not paying you until I'm happy with it!

ME: You've already paid us for it.

CLIENT: I'm going to take you to court.

ME: Bring it.

Seeing Red

"We can't put so much red in the logo and on the packaging; my sister's going through menopause right now."

Your One Phone Call

"Hi, sorry I haven't gotten back to you. I've been in jail for a few days. I don't want to talk about why. I really shouldn't be calling you—they've got people everywhere. I might be hard to get a hold of for awhile. Can I get your address again, so I can send your payment? Also, I might need a place to, uh, crash for a few days when I get out, if that's cool."

A client called me in a panic from his annual holiday in France:

> CLIENT: I have an urgent problem...
> ME: Okay, what's up?
> CLIENT: Well, there's something up with my site and I need you to fix it immediately. I've just pulled it up from the villa and the whole site is coming up in English not French.
> ME: That's correct; it's an English website.
> CLIENT [*now very irate*]: I know, but I'm in France! The site should be in French when I log on from France, so that French people can read what I do!

"Can you make it so the graphics go 'woosh'?"
[*The client starts making a sound not dissimilar to a light saber...*]

When redesigning a magazine website...

> CLIENT: I want you to bury all the links for the magazine at the bottom of the page.
> ME: Wait, you don't want them in the nav bar? At all?
> CLIENT: No, I want the product guide to be the only thing that matters.
> ME: What happens if someone comes to the site to subscribe to the magazine?
> CLIENT: Fuck 'em.
> *A year later the magazine folded.*

Underwhelming

CLIENT: You're fired.
ME: Why?
CLIENT: You printed the sign upside-down.
ME: Nope, you're just holding it upside-down.

After I completed 85% of a client's website, he ignored my emails for six months and dodged my invoices. Then, one day he called...

CLIENT: Hey, man, I need to talk to you about getting the site finished.
ME: Man, it's been six months since I've heard from you. We met for coffee, you said you would send me your photos and you haven't been in touch since.
CLIENT: Yeah, I've been busy. But we need to get those testimonials done.
ME: Dude, I've got a full-time job, no time, and you owe me money. The site is up in a test directory on your server. I'll send you the .PSDs and we'll just call it even. You can find someone else to finish the last two pages. I'm too busy.
CLIENT: Yeah? You're busy? I'm busy. My grandmother died and then, man, a house fell on my tree!
ME: A house fell on your tree?
CLIENT: Yes! So, man, don't tell me you're busy!
ME: Let's just call this even. The contract said 60 days without contact caused a breach. We're good. Use the money you were going to pay me to just pay someone else. Everything's fair.
CLIENT: Oh yeah? We'll see. It'll cost you... I'm taking you to court, MOTHERFUCKER! You'll pay. You'll see how it is. You'll see.

Forbidden Website

CLIENT: You need to look at my site—China is on it.
ME: What do you mean?
CLIENT: I went to my site and China is on it.
ME: You mean it's been hacked?
CLIENT: I don't know, but China is on there and I need you to get them off.

A conversation with a female client:

> **CLIENT:** I want teal as the overall color.
> **ME:** Okay, we can go with PMS 320.
> **CLIENT:** Do you think you're funny? What are you insinuating by referring to teal as "PMS?" Maybe a female designer wouldn't find teal as humorous as you do.

"Why do you keep using big words like 'anomaly'? I've never met a designer with a large vocabulary. It's irritating."

Birdbrain

A client asked me to create a logo for his auto shop. I asked him to describe the type of auto work his shop did so I could come up with a theme for the logo. He told me it was your general auto work: tune-ups, replacement of faulty parts and engine maintenance.

He then insisted that the logo include a chicken.

> **ME:** Wait, what? Why? Your business has nothing to do with chickens. The name of your workshop is [*Name*]. It has ABSOLUTELY nothing to do with chickens.
> **CLIENT:** I know, but, well, what can I say? I LOVE CHICKENS.

We were presenting several print concepts to a national milk board, promoting milk as a healthy drink. For obvious reasons, a few of our concepts featured cows, to which the client said, "No, no, no—we can't show cows in our ads. Our customers will find it disgusting when they realize that milk comes from cows."

It's All Relative

After seven frustrating attempts to teach our client how to insert products into his virtual store, I patiently sat down with him and asked him what he didn't understand.

CLIENT: Everything.

ME: But have you actually tried to insert a product? Have you tried reading the instruction booklet I wrote for you?

CLIENT: No.

ME: Well, I'll show you one more time and then you should try doing it yourself. It's not difficult. I'm sure you'll nail it on your first try.

CLIENT: Hey, missy, what the hell are you implying? I'm more intelligent than you, your boss and everyone else at this company combined! I'm smarter than Einstein and more talented than Tom Cruise! Just because I suffered childhood traumas that prevent me from managing my virtual store, doesn't make me any less of a genius than I really am!

It's Just Not Clicking

CLIENT: Can you click the picture?

ME: No. What do you want it to do? Enlarge?

CLIENT: No, I just want to click it.

ME: But when you click it, what do you want to happen?

CLIENT: I just want to be able to click it!

ME: And what version of Windows are you using?

CLIENT: Look, pal. I know two things about this fucking computer: I paid a lot of fucking money for it and it doesn't fucking work.

"I'm not here to buy you a new car, pal!"

"If this situation is not rectified, I will be issuing a worldwide press release via online mediums, social networks and fax."

ME: How can we demonstrate that your product is better than the competing products?

CLIENT: What, are you calling me a liar?

CLIENT: So here's the deal: my company gave me $7,000 for this project, but since you only charged us $3500, why don't you just write me a receipt for $7,000 and I'll split the balance with you?

ME: I don't know, that doesn't seem right.

CLIENT: Fuck you! Are you threatening me?

"Hate it. Try again."

CIRCLE VI — HERESY

Oh, ye [client] of little faith. Why did you hire me if you don't believe in what I'm doing?

If you've ever asked yourself this question, it's likely because you've been working with a client who is guilty of heresy. This Client From Hell questions your every move, convinced that they can do it better than you can or that you're simply doing it wrong. These clients assume that just because the things you do are new and unfamiliar to them, you're the dummy who needs to reread the user's manual. In a nutshell, these clients don't believe in what you're doing at all, and thus make it their full-time job to challenge you at every turn.

CLIENTS FROM HELL

The Prophet

"Oh, the product will sell. God wants it to."

We were pitching a potential client on a new website. When we mentioned we should hire a photographer for a half-day shoot, he replied, "Well, I got a Canon Rebel for Christmas and I'm pretty good with it."

"I understand that you prefer to use Photoshop, but we don't feel that it's a universal enough program. If you could do all of the design work in Microsoft Paint, it would be easier for us to edit it and give you an idea of the changes we want."

CLIENT: Four hundred dollars for a logo? Why are you so expensive? My nephew has Photoshop—I can just get him to do it.
ME: Does your nephew have Microsoft Word?
CLIENT: Yes.
ME: Then have him write you a novel while he's at it.

"You don't need to go to art school to know that blue and yellow don't go together."

Well, if it ain't the ol' "websites are free" argument...

"I need a website, FAST. I want it set up so that I can add, edit and delete content when I need to, and I need it done as soon as possible. How do we go about doing this? Obviously it shouldn't cost that much, as there are so many free websites available these days."

"I took a marketing course, so I'd like to submit some of my own ideas. The business cards have far too much wasted space so I want to add a calendar to the back—people will love it and use it all the time. The newspaper ad is fine, but I'd like you to get them to print it upside down; that way people will instinctively want to rotate the newspaper to read it. Pretty good ideas, don't you think?"

CLIENT: This is absolutely wrong. Where's all of the HTML? We want the HTML.

ME: I don't understand. All the files should be on the flash drive we gave you yesterday.

CLIENT: Well, what's all this PHP jumbo-mumbo?

ME: PHP is just a language. It does all the work for your CMS. You can't have CMS with only HTML files.

CLIENT: I get it. You just don't understand. WEBSITES. ARE. MADE. OF. H-T-M-L. Or did you not learn that at whatever school you went to?

ME: I didn't go to college.

CLIENT: I'm working with a bunch of idiots.

"We can't put this children's game on our site because it uses dice. Dice are also used for gambling, and gambling is a sin."

Whiteboard
After presenting a new design for a company website, the owner leaned over, asked if she could suggest some changes and started drawing the changes on my MacBook's screen with a black marker.

Counting Your Losses
"Well, I was hoping you wouldn't just be interested in making money. I wanted you to understand how much you could learn from me, and how valuable that would be. That's why I think $12/hour is a fair rate for you to produce the website. If you can't work at this rate, then you simply miss out."

CLIENT: Oh, wow, this looks GREAT! But seriously, we want to be original here.

ME: Oh, I'm sorry. When we discussed the design together, you made it seem as though this is what you wanted—is there something that you would like me to change?

CLIENT: No, no. The idea is fine; it's just that it's pretty obvious you traced that.

ME: No, I didn't. This is an original illustration I created specifically for your company.

CLIENT: Come on, even *I* can't draw that well. I know you traced it!

An Offer You Can't Refuse
A form-response I received after applying for a graphic design vacancy:

Dear [Me],

Thanks for your reply and interest in the position of print designer with [name of company]. If successful, you will be expected to work a three-month, pro bono probationary period and will spend three days per week laboring on-site with our construction workers. It is possible that you will have to design the website during your lunch breaks, also on-site. It's okay, though—the van is very comfortable. But you will have to buy a laptop.

Let us know ASAP.

Regards, [Employer]

The Forbidden Fruit

CLIENT: Hey, just one final question before I send the deposit: Do you use a PC or a Mac?

ME: I use a Mac.

CLIENT: That's a problem. Do you have access to a PC? I'm not a supporter of Apple products.

ME: No, I don't have access to a PC, but this will have little to no effect on the work itself.

CLIENT: I'm a Christian and Apple products are sinful. You need only look at their logo, an apple with a bite taken from it. Do you not know the story of Adam and Eve in the Garden of Eden? If I allowed you to create my website on a Mac, I would be just like Adam, taking a bite of the forbidden fruit. [*Silence*]

Take my advice: destroy your Mac and repent for when judgment day comes. It shall be you who is cast to hell for your sins.

CLIENT: Oh, man, I think $500 for the logo is way too expensive.

ME: Well, that's my rate, but my work is guaranteed.

CLIENT: Mmm, I don't know. I just don't think a logo should cost more than 50 bucks.

ME: For 50 bucks, I'll draw you some doodles on a napkin.

CLIENT: Great, can you fax it to me?

"Your designs are too pretty, too beautiful looking. I need them to look more like I designed them. For example, instead of using a green box to highlight a chunk of copy, I would put green trees all over the page. You should try and be more creative like me and stop trying to make everything look so good all of the time."

CLIENT: We like the design, but could you make the blues all the same?

ME: It's the same blue throughout the design.

CLIENT: It looks like different blues.

ME: That's because colors are perceived differently depending on their neighboring colors.

CLIENT: That's stupid.

"I don't care if we lose 90% of our visitors; we can't have a 'skip' option on the flash intro. We paid a lot of money for that, so everybody has to see it."

CLIENT: I want you to do a three-minute animation for my website. It's okay if it's in Flash. How much is that?

ME: That depends, what did you have in mind exactly?

CLIENT: Well, I don't know. It depends on how much it costs.

ME: The price depends on how complex the designs are. Things such as the level of interactivity, whether we need to license music, if we need voiceovers, etc.

CLIENT: I'm just asking how much three minutes of animation is. I don't know what I want.

ME: Well, the most basic designs start at $3,000 and more complex designs are upwards of $20,000.

CLIENT: WHAT? I thought it would be like $100. I told you: you can do it in Flash.

ME: That's how much Flash animation costs.

CLIENT: Bullshit. I know Flash does all the animating for you.

CLIENT: We like the green, but it's just a little *too* green. Can you use our green?

ME: That is your green.

CLIENT: Oh, well it looks more lime-y. We want it more like our green.

ME: The lime green is your green. It is exactly what you have on your logo.

CLIENT: Oh, okay. Well then, can you change it by one?

ME: One what? Do you want it lighter or darker?

CLIENT: No, just change it by one.

CLIENT: The logo looks great, but can we change the address font to Arabic? I need it for my Middle Eastern viewers.

ME: Arabic is just the name of the font. It doesn't actually change the words into another language. I can purchase an actual Arabic font, and have it translated into Arabic if you want.

CLIENT: So, Times New Roman doesn't change the words to Italian?

ME: No, Times New Roman is just a standard...

CLIENT: Are you sure? Let me call you back after I check Word 2009. I have the newest version, so maybe it only does it in the newer version. I'll give you a call back later today.

Nowadays, employers seem to think that all graphic design work is done by software and that designers are just doing data-entry. I've even seen job offers that refer to graphic artists as "computer operators," rather than as trained and (hopefully) experienced design professionals.

A few years ago, however, art directors and account managers had more respect for the skills of their artists. Well, sometimes...

It was a Friday afternoon, ten minutes before quitting time, when the account team at the major ad agency where I worked raced into my studio. They ran directly to my desk and dropped a handful of paintings and photos in front of me.

"We need your help, but we promise it'll only take an hour."

I understand advertising deadlines, and I was the "go-to" guy when jobs were on the line.

"Sure," I said. "Whatchya got?"

They showed me an illustration: a painting of a man in a rowboat on a lake, with the wake of the boat spelling out the name of their product. They also showed me some photos torn from magazines, which were probably reference pictures for the painting: lakes, men in boats, that sort of thing.

"We commissioned this illustration," they explained, "and we decided we want to give the client a non-illustrated option—a real photo. But we have to ship the ads to the printer and we don't have time to set up a shoot, so we want you to create a photo using these magazine pictures. It has to be ready to release, so you have to make it really polished—and make it sharper and hi-res."

"You realize that even if I can do this, it'll take about 12 hours, and there's no guarantee I can make it look like a real photo."

"Yes, you can. You have Photoshop!" The art director screamed.

One of the account guys then quietly confirmed everything I said.

"Listen," I said. "You have a finished illustration. If you really want me to do this, I can, but I can't have it done until tomorrow—and that's only if I stay all night. My guess is that your illustration will still look better than what I come up with."

Here, the art director blew his stack:

"LOOK; THIS WON'T TAKE MORE THAN TWO HOURS! I'D DO IT MYSELF IF I KNEW HOW TO USE PHOTOSHOP!"

"I've decided that you billed us far too much. Here's my thinking: We're paying you to come up with an idea, not for the time it takes you to think about it. The actual idea must only take about 30 seconds to come up with. All these visuals, they're just typing. I can do that in Word. It would take me five minutes. So, I only want to pay you for five and a half minutes of work."

"Well I'm a bit of a designer myself. I have a MySpace."

"Let's negotiate on the price. Don't forget, my wife can do this for free."

CLIENT: I need you to illustrate 360 jokes for my book.
ME: Okay, what's your budget?
CLIENT: I don't have much; I can pay [*nominal amount of money*].
ME: That works out to be less than minimum wage for the time it will take me.
CLIENT: Well, that's okay. You probably do this stuff for fun anyway, right? Artists just sit around drawing for hours working on this stuff for kicks.
ME: Sir, I do this for a living.

[*click*]

Four More Words I Hate
"This will be easy."

"Instead of designing icons and costing me extra, why don't you just use the 'Wingdings' font?"

CLIENT: We like your proposal and enthusiasm, but we really can't afford you. How much would you charge to rent out your computer?

ME: Excuse me?

CLIENT: Our sales manager is pretty creative. We could just have him come to your office on a Saturday and knock this thing out.

ME: So, you don't want to hire me, but you want to rent my computer??

CLIENT: Yeah. And you could be there. You know, to give him some tips if he gets stuck. Maybe toss in a creative idea or two. In fact, we'll do all of the work and still use your creative ideas. It's a win-win!

After handing a client an invoice for a rather large rebrand job…

CLIENT: The problem with this is that you're one of those freeloaders, aren't you?

ME: Freeloader? Do you mean freelancer?

CLIENT: No, you're a freeloader. You went through university to learn all this artsy-fartsy stuff on my hard-earned taxes. Let's just go ahead and call this work a repayment.

CLIENT: I don't want to use non-moving navigation buttons. Static buttons are going the way of the dinosaur.

ME: What would you like me to use then?

CLIENT: A looping movie where the customer has to click on the fast-moving objects to navigate through the site. It will keep them on their toes.

Hieroglyphics

ME: The typeface we used for the headlines is Bodoni.

CLIENT: It doesn't look very readable.

ME: Well, it's set at 18 point and has been used as a face for over 200 years. It's known for its legibility.

CLIENT: You can't fool me; fonts didn't exist back then!

Novel Idea

"Please be sure to print the cover and the table of contents at the front of the book. And after the table of contents, print the chapters in this order: 1,2,3,4,5,6,7,8,9,10,11,12,13,14,15,16."

CLIENT: What's your rate?
ME: Fifty dollars an hour.
CLIENT: Can I come watch you?
ME: Sure, for $100 an hour.
CLIENT: What if I help you?
ME: That'll be $400 an hour.

CLIENT: I studied design, so basically I know what I want.
ME: Cool, what do you want?
CLIENT: You're the designer; you come up with the idea. But for your sake, it better match up with my idea.

"Why so much? My nephew works on computers at Best Buy and makes $12 an hour."

CLIENT: What paint software are you using at the moment?
ME: It's called Photoshop CS4, but it's more than just paint software.
CLIENT: Could you make me a copy of it for my 6-year-old son to mess around on? He likes painting.
ME: Er... No, that's piracy and it's licensed to me and my company.
CLIENT: I'll provide you with a disc.
ME: The issue here is greater than my lack of a disk.
CLIENT: Yeah, it's me reconsidering your final fee.

CLIENT: We need the site to be deeply spiritual. The use of a cross is obvious and perhaps overused, but we would like to go with it. Also, perhaps some saints, figurines, etc… Do you get the idea?

ME: Do you have any specific saints in mind?

CLIENT: No, just run with it. After all, we all worship the same God, right?

ME: Actually, no; I'm atheist. Is that a problem?"

CLIENT: Oh, you´re one of them, are you? That is indeed a problem. People who abandon the word of God are in league with the Devil. If you designed our site, well, it would make it sinful—a place of deception. Perhaps we should discuss your hatred of God, so I can convince you of the true path."

ME: I cannot hate something that doesn't exist.

CLIENT: I see. We're going to need a designer who is, you know, not in bed with the devil.

"After taking the time to explain my project I would think that you would be courteous enough to say, 'Sorry, Mike, I can't help you.' I consider a person like you quite capable of sharing trade secrets. I'm sending you this email to create a record, and advise you not to share the information that I provided to you."

"Because I have been placing all of my focus on this project I have fallen out of touch with our Almighty God and Jesus Christ. I have made myself susceptible to the Evil One, Satan. I can tell you, I have been seeing signs of this these past months."

CIRCLE VII — VIOLENCE

A rare, but always crowd-pleasing tactic in the Client From Hell's arsenal of torture is violence. Not just the physical kind, though—client violence comes in all shapes and sizes: hostility, emotionally-abusive insults, racism, homophobia, the punching of inanimate objects, physical assault, cat-sacrifices, etc. The only thing that will make them more pissed off than your responding in kind is your not responding at all. Unfortunately, very few of us are up to this sadistic challenge.

After three months without hearing from a client...

CLIENT: Okay, let's get this site finished!

ME: Sure, I'm fully booked at the moment but I'd be happy to book you in for the end of next month.

CLIENT: What are you talking about? Let's get this done by Friday!

ME: Like I said, I'm fully booked with other clients at the moment, but I can block out some time for you at the end of next month.

CLIENT: Are you fucking joking? I fucking paid you your fucking money to do this site. I come first!

ME: Well, I'm afraid that as I haven't heard from you for three months, I did have to take on some other clients in order to actually keep my business running. I can't just blow them off, and you actually haven't paid me in full. You have an outstanding invoice for £500.

CLIENT: That's not fucking good enough.

ME: I'm really sorry, that's the best I can do.

CLIENT: How about I come round there and kick your fucking head in? Would that move things along?

ME: I'm afraid not, no.

A phone call from a client's administrative assistant...

ASSISTANT: So, uh, [client] didn't really like the Photoshop filter you used on that image.

ME: Okay, no problem. I'll try something else.

ASSISTANT: Well, actually, he said he was going to do it himself instead.

ME: Do it himself?

ASSISTANT: Yes — I know, it doesn't really make much sense, but he was kind of freaking out about it. He, err, punched a hole in the wall, actually. And, well — I don't want to suggest he's unstable or anything, but if your doorbell rings any time in the next few minutes, you probably shouldn't answer it.

"Please remove the images of black people. Our clients are all white."

New Screensaver?

A local fruit juice client contacted me to help him with a rebranding project. He came to my office and presented a storyboard of his vision for the introductory animation of his website. The first few slides showed a banana, a pineapple, a peach and a strawberry happily dancing and cheering as they walk around in circles. About three or four slides in, the fruits all jump into a working blender as their juices splatter all over the screen. This is then followed by a slow fade-in of the company logo.

Misery Loves Company

"We like the design, we like the layout, we like everything except for the photos. The seniors look a little too happy and independent. Can we find photos of seniors that look more depressed please? This needs to be authentic."

Watch Out for the Gays

We were building a website for a preschool, and just before we went live our client requested we remove the word "school" from all the page titles and URLs. When I asked why, the client responded:

"We heard that if the gays find out we have a preschool, they can force us to teach the children to be gay. We think it's safest if nobody can see that we're a school. And we don't want to come up on any Google searches for 'school' either."

Not Quite Black Enough

CLIENT: You know the picture of the black man on the homepage?
ME: Yeah, I know the one. What about it?
CLIENT: Well, it's just that he's not quite black enough. We want a shiny black man on the homepage.

"All the artwork is approved, but we need to replace the skeleton. We think it might be homosexual and could therefore alienate the audience. We work in a very masculine industry."

After reviewing a 2-inch square business card proof…

"When I get a business card like this, I assume the person is a fag."

And another time…

"Can you make my business card less gay looking?"

Stupid or Racist: Pick One

A very difficult and picky client was looking for voiceover talent. She did not want to pay very much, but wanted someone "who sounds like James Earl Jones."

By some miracle, the talent company found someone who sounded almost exactly like the real James Earl Jones. I excitedly played the clip for the client. Her response? "Ewww. No. He sounds black."

In response to an illustration in an educational book on hygiene for an NGO in a developing country:

"We don't want to show a father bathing his child. It implies incest."

ME: So, in what languages do you want to release this game?
CLIENT: All of the major ones: English, German, Arabic, French, Spanish...
ME: What about Chinese? Don't you want to reach consumers in Asia?
CLIENT: Yeah, but I assume that any Chinese person who can afford an iPhone can also speak English.

Following a pleasant phone conversation with a client, he told me he hoped I wasn't homosexual, because my site looked "a bit gay with the pink."

"Pop in a dark kid, an Asian or a kid with glasses from time to time."

"These stock photos of Native Americans don't look very Native American. Can we try Filipinos?"

"I don't want gay people looking at the site! Can you do it with CSS3?"

"Those hands look like lesbian hands."

Upon the client's review of his new logo:

"I love the overall look, but I want to ni**er it up some."

Yep, he totally dropped the N-bomb.

"Well, you just made a terrible mistake. We don't want black or Hispanic people in our ads. I'm sorry if this sounds racist, but we are."

When designing a website for a client, he expressed his desire to use burgundy. I obliged.

CLIENT: This isn't right. You know the color blood red?
ME: Yeah, I think I know what you're talking about.
CLIENT: Yeah, I love blood red. I want the logo to look like that. Do you know what it would look like if you took a paintbrush, dipped it in blood and smeared it downwards? How the blood would be darkest in the center, and there would be splatters of blood and lighter shades of blood around it?
ME: You want a gradient?
CLIENT: No, I want it to look like the blood of all our victims.
ME: I'm sorry, what?
CLIENT: You know, from all the bugs we've terminated.
ME: Oh.

Put It in Writing
An email from a client:

"I'm not threatening you, but just know that I am going to make your life a living HELL. I will make you suffer. Mark my words: you're putting your health at risk."

CLIENT: What if we showed a picture of an old plantation with slaves in chains in the front yard? We could call it "Plantation Strike Gin." Do you think the coloreds would mind?
ME: Uh, yeah. I also think I would mind.

CLIENT: I'm looking for someone to take over the build-out of our website.
ME: Not a problem.
CLIENT: But before we get any further…are you Chinese?
ME: I'm sorry?
CLIENT: I don't work with the Chinese. The guy before you was Chinese and I found him to be very selfish and greedy. I paid for his dinner every night, and he got upset with me when I asked him to pay for my dinner one time.
ME: Um, no. I'm not Chinese.
CLIENT: Good. I don't like them.
ME: Yeah, you mentioned.

An eyeglass company wanted me to create six different 3-D heads of various shapes and races, so they could illustrate the right method of picking out new frames. When I presented my mock-ups to them, they were pleased with all of them, except for the black one.

CLIENT: That guy looks TOO black. Like Sambo. Can you make him look less black?
[*Irritated, I took the white man and changed his skin color to a light brown.*]
CLIENT: Perfect! Now he looks like a nice black guy.

You know what's really great to come across when looking for a pen in a client's desk drawer? A handgun.

A client sent a caricature of himself for use in an advertisement I was creating for his business.

CLIENT: Would it be possible for you to get rid of my mustache in that drawing?
ME: Sure, that shouldn't be a problem.
CLIENT: Good. I don't want anyone thinking I'm one of those A-rabs.

CLIENT: I'm running for office and I've heard you're an excellent photographer. I'd like to have you take my photograph for my upcoming campaign.
ME: That sounds great! I'd love to meet and find out mo….
CLIENT: Actually, let me tell you about myself right now! I'm a family man… And I! DO! NOT! LIKE! GAYS! Get my drift?
ME: Oh, my.

"I'd like you to use a stock photo for this piece. Choose something with a group of people in it. Just no black people."

Take my project or else!

"We are a kickboxing gym and we need a website to advertise our classes. We previously had a web designer, but he could not finish the project and is now in the hospital. Can you help?"

CIRCLE VIII — FRAUD

Fraudulent clients might not be the most prevalent of our cast of characters, but their cuts often run the deepest. That's because they tend to very sinisterly and simultaneously jeopardize your time and your money. You see, the fraudulent client has a simple approach to life: get as much out of it with as little expense possible. After all, why buy the design cow when you can get that delicious design milk for free?

CLIENTS FROM HELL

Five words you don't want to hear from a prospect:
"I'm pretty broke right now."

"Can you bill your time in six-minute increments?"

When DIY Becomes "Do It for Me"
"I already have a design in mind, so implementing it should be easy for you if you're a good designer. Just know that I'd totally build this myself if I had the time. It's very straightforward, so I expect to not have to pay for this."

Exchange Rate
"You're gonna charge $400 for that? Aren't you from India? What are you going to do with $400?!"

"I know you said it would take three weeks but I've just looked at my budget and I can't pay you after today—so you need to finish everything by 5 p.m."

I did $75 worth of production work for a client's friend. After going three months without payment, I finally received a check in the mail for $7.50 with a note that said, "1 of 10."

Supermarket Rate

CLIENT: Can you design a poster calendar for our company?
ME: Sure.
CLIENT: Since the price per calendar is about 2.50 € in the supermarket; I will pay you 4 € for the design.

After spending some time with a potential client interested in web design work, I finally asked him about his budget for the project. His response was, "Oh, actually I won't be paying you. I thought you wouldn't mind working for the networking opportunities."

"It's so good to finally meet you. Thank you very much for coming. We have no money."

CLIENT: We're not moving forward with the project—the shopping cart doesn't meet our needs.
ME: Okay, but there's still a balance due on the project that needs to be paid.
CLIENT: We don't see it that way, so we're not paying.
ME: Completed work does need to be paid for.
CLIENT: Again, we don't see it that way.

CLIENT: I want you to develop two logos for me. What's your rate?
ME: Great, my rate's $250 per logo. But I understand you're just starting up and I would be able to cut you a deal if that's out of your range.
CLIENT: What's "a deal"?
ME: How about $200 total for both logos?
CLIENT: I can't really afford that. What if I gave you $50, and mowed your lawn?

In a contract I received from a client:

"If payment for services is not received, all work must still be completed."

ME: I'll send over your invoice today.
CLIENT: Oh…you want to be paid?

"Okay, the horse lost. Can I pay you in cocaine?"

KGB :: IOU

"We're well known among all the Russian billionaires so there's great potential for you to get your name out there by doing this project for free. Also, I am a direct descendant of Genghis Khan."

Client's rationale for not needing to pay for the poster and website design for his event:

"Our festival isn't about money—it's about bringing people together."

"I can't afford to pay you the balance, but would you like my Jack Russell Terrier?"

CLIENT: How much do you charge for a website?
ME: Well, it depends.
CLIENT: Can you just give us a ballpark figure?
ME: Professional or minor league?

Maybe the Tossed Kind

"Can we pay for the logo in installments, or even better, can I pay you in salad?"

Sales Technique

After delivering an e-commerce site to a client, he called me to say he'd experienced some problems ordering products. While on the phone with him, I placed a test order to see if I could reconstruct the problem he encountered. The ordering went fine, but…

> **CLIENT:** Wow, I just got an order from you. You want that Jacuzzi? I'd suggest [*some Jacuzzi name*] instead!
>
> **ME:** Ha, that's funny. But yeah, that was just a test order. I definitely don't want a Jacuzzi.
>
> **CLIENT:** Well, you ordered one, now you have to pay. I'll just take it off your invoice.

> **ME:** The total price of the project is $2,500—I can either take a deposit of 10% upfront and you can pay the balance upon delivery OR I can discount the entire project by 10% if you pay in advance.
>
> **CLIENT:** I'll take the discount and pay it all in advance.
>
> **ME:** Great, then I'll plan to get started as soon as I receive your payment.
>
> **CLIENT:** Oh, I'll pay you when it's done. Don't you trust me?
>
> **ME:** I thought you wanted to pay in advance so that you could get the discount.
>
> **CLIENT:** I do! I'll pay in advance once the job is completed!

"But I thought you were a FREE-lancer?!"

ME: The cost starts at [*amount*] per illustration, but can vary slightly depending on the project.

CLIENT: What do you mean by "it can vary"? Can you give me an example?

ME: I usually offer a 10% discount if you order more than 10 illustrations. Or, for example, my last client was a nonprofit, so I gave them a 20% discount.

CLIENT: Oh, really? That's interesting because, umm, we're a nonprofit, too. I mean, not right now, but we're definitely planning to give away free stuff to, umm, urban kids and umm, help them out, y'know...?

AIRLINE CLIENT: You quoted us for eight days of 2D graphics. I think that's way too much.

ME: It includes revisions.

AIRLINE CLIENT: Well, if you do everything perfectly and we don't want to change anything, can you charge us less?

ME: If your airline flew us to London and got us there 10 minutes ahead of schedule, would everyone on the plane get a refund?

A chocolate coin company emailed me asking for a quote for a new website. I told them my price, and they replied, "Can we just pay in chocolate coins? They're better than real money, and they've got chocolate ganache inside, too!"

Craigslist Ad

I have a once-in-a-lifetime opportunity for the right designer. Your job will be to help me build the next Twitter, so you will need to be an expert at:

- Web design and graphics
- Website systems and programming
- Getting ranked first on Google
- Generating one million visitors per month

This is an intern position and does not pay, but you will be able to put this on your resume and get great exposure!

Working Vacation

While reviewing a quote for a rush job that would require working through the weekend, the client commented that paying extra seemed wrong. His exact words:

"I'm giving you a break from your family for two days—why should I pay for that?"

CLIENT: Fifty dollars? That's kind of steep, don't you think?
ME: No, the project will take me about two hours.
CLIENT: Well, what's your hourly rate? I need to save money.
ME: $25 an hour.
CLIENT: That's much better. I think we can work with that.

As a favor to a colleague, I offered to help his friend develop the look and feel of his new product. In return, he would treat me to lunch every few weeks when we met to discuss our ideas. When the project got to a point where significant design and engineering were needed, I presented the friend with a contract, and asked if he would like me to continue with his project.

CLIENT: That's too much; I can't afford it. You know, you'll get a lot of money when the product sells millions.
ME: I'm sorry, but I can't work on speculation. I really can't work further on your project without a contract in place, stating that I will get paid for my design and engineering work.
CLIENT: It's too much. But I'd like to invite you to my house on Saturday.
ME: For…? Is there a special occasion?
CLIENT: I just want to show you how poor I am as proof that I have no money to pay your fees.

Antonyms: Cheap, Soon

ME: What's your budget?
CLIENT: ACAP.
ME: Care to elaborate?
CLIENT: As Cheap As Possible… Oh, and ASAP!

CLIENT: So, how much does a logo cost?

ME: It depends—usually around [price].

CLIENT: What if I said that I'm actually Haitian—would you do it for free?

"It seems as though every time we ask you to do any work, we have to pay for it."

"You'll never make any money if you're always charging for every little thing you do!"

ME: Your invoice is nearly 90 days overdue.

CLIENT: We'll pay you when our client pays us. Stop asking for loans—we're not a bank!

CLIENT: I was thinking I could pay you in groceries.

ME [*laughing*]: You're joking, right?

CLIENT: I don't get what's so hilarious here.

ME: I apologize, but honestly, that's one of the most ridiculous methods of payment I've been offered.

CLIENT: Really? I think it's quite sane.

ME: Well, are you talking about a grocery store gift card?

CLIENT: No, I just came into a wealth of about $300 worth of carrots and $450 of potatoes.

CLIENT: The logo looks awesome—thanks! We're going to go with it!

ME: Great, I'll put the high-res files on a CD and drop it off to your office this afternoon. You can write me a check then.

CLIENT: Yeah, I wanted to talk to you about that. We think that instead of a traditional payment, we're going to put you on the barter system.

ME: But you agreed to my costs weeks ago.

CLIENT: Wouldn't you like a new TV instead? We could get you one. Or maybe one of our other suppliers could fix your guttering or something?

ME: I already have a TV—a new one isn't going to feed my family. I'll take a check as agreed.

CLIENT: But the barter system has been around, like, forever. You scratch my back, I scratch yours.

ME: Okay, tell you what, instead of paying me, you can come around to my house and cook me dinner every night for a month.

CLIENT: …

ME: Hello?

CLIENT: So how much do I make the check out for?

ME: Great meeting! Now that you've seen our progress and understand that we're doing things better than our competitors, let's talk about the $4,700 payment.

CLIENT: I've been carrying your check around in my wallet. Really, you can see from the creases how long I have been carrying it for you.

ME: Great, but the check isn't made out to me.

CLIENT: Well, give it back to me and I'll make it out for $1,000— business has been really bad for me.

ME: You realize that will only cover part of what I paid out of pocket to the coders in India, and they expect me to come back from this meeting with additional payment because of our progress.

CLIENT: Hmm, well, I have a hat you can have.

[The client hands me a hat that reads "blood donor."]

CLIENT: Chicks dig it.

Potty Mouth

ME: Hi. I'm checking to see if you received the invoice I sent over. We're going on almost four months now and we'd appreciate your payment.

CLIENT: Yes, I received it, but I'm not going to pay it yet.

ME: Why's that? Was there a problem?

CLIENT: No problem. I just haven't used your designs yet, so I'll pay you when once I do.

ME: Listen, I really need you to pay the invoice. Our terms are due upon receipt as we discussed.

CLIENT: I'm not sure when I will need to start using your designs, but when I do I'll pay you. Don't worry.

ME: Yeah, well, we did the work and we need to get paid regardless of if or when you use it. If a plumber fixes your toilet, you don't tell him you will pay as soon as you take a shit, do you?

CLIENT: That's disgusting! My bathroom habits are none of your business and as soon as I use what you sent me, you will get paid!

CLIENT: What's this invoice for?

ME: That's the initial deposit; you pay it to start the project and ensure my time commitment to you.

CLIENT: I can't pay this; I don't have any money.

ME: Umm, okay, then I can't build you a website.

CLIENT: But you agreed to. I signed your agreement!

ME: I think there's been a misunderstanding. You agreed to my terms, which include paying an upfront deposit. We talked about this. You said money was no object.

CLIENT: Oh, yes, well, I meant money's no object after the website is built and I've sold all my sculptures. I can't pay you anything now. I want you to build me a free site, and when I'm rich, I'll pay you.

"Hey, sorry to call you on your holiday. My boss has found out about me running a business on the side and has blocked me from accessing my webmail. I just need you to log in and read some emails to me."

"I don't know what you do, how you do it or how long it takes, but I am not paying your damn invoice."

"You know, with the economy and all…"

"I need a web design portfolio site, but have no time to do it myself. I'm looking for someone who is fairly skilled at web design. The better the outcome, the more I'll pay."

"We shouldn't have to pay you for this because if we had the resources in-house, we'd be able to do it for free."

CIRCLE IX — BETRAYAL

The Client From Hell who indulges in betrayal views no promise as so absolute, no contract as so airtight, and no relationship meaningful enough that it can't be broken, reneged on, or otherwise abandoned in pursuit of selfish goals and gains. The Betraying Client cloaks his attacks in niceties such as interest, gratitude and genuine encouragement. Put simply, Betraying Clients are bearers of imbalance and have mastered the art of taking without giving.

CLIENTS FROM HELL

CLIENT: For our new logo, don't use any images of hands, and we like neutral colors like browns and beiges.
ME: No problem.
[*I submit three concepts.*]
CLIENT: Actually, we like this logo that our son designed.

The logo is an illustration of a pair of hands, in blue.

Have you ever had a client ask you for both a detailed proposal and the contact info for a freelancer who's cheaper than you?

I was working late one night to launch a website I'd been working on for a few months. After putting up all of the files, I decided I would text message the client to let him know the site was live.

TEXT MESSAGE TO CLIENT: Website is launched.
TEXT MESSAGE FROM CLIENT: Okay, great. Now that the site is launched I wanted to let you know that these past few months have been terrible. You are a bit difficult to work with. I will not be paying your final invoice. Sorry.

Obviously I high-tailed it back to the server and deleted all of the files. Sorry.

"We've decided not to use any of the concepts you proposed. Instead, we farmed this out to our creative network, and have decided to use a rotating set of 50 different clip-art images as our logo."

Great Work

"I'm very happy with the website, and so excited to get this launched so we can move forward with our careers. By the way, if you don't get these last set of changes done within the next few weeks, I'm going to hire a new set of developers and deduct 50% of whatever their costs are from your final payment. I think that's completely fair."

CLIENT: I'm looking for a complete line of custom coffee labels designed for my new line of coffee. There will be 50 labels in total. How much do you charge and how long would something like this take?

[After lengthy evaluation, proposal and time estimate...]

CLIENT: That is just ridiculous! Why would I pay anyone that much money and why will it take so long? I'm going to tell everyone that you charge way too much money and that you're a waste of time.

ME: I'm sorry you feel that way. That's really all I can offer you at this time.

CLIENT: I'm pretty sure I can hire a high school student to do this for me for $15 an hour.

A client wanted us to design an e-commerce site. We asked if she had a budget, and she said, "No, it costs what it costs." My partner and I proposed a very reasonable price, and in the proposal we stated that any additional work would be billed at $60 per hour. She refused to even look at the proposal, handing it off to one of the interns to "deal with."

After three months of work, we still hadn't been paid for our initial invoice. We called the client, who assured us that her intern was handling it and that we would get a check in the mail. About a week later, we still hadn't heard from the intern. So, we did what we usually do in this situation: halted work and sent a note saying as much. The client phoned me after receiving the message, basically screaming at me that it was too expensive. She said, "You shouldn't have spent more than 10 hours designing and programming it; I don't want to spend more than $600."

We had spent 10 hours in meetings alone.

"We like the site, but our creative director has decided that he wants it built in flash. There's some debate as to whether we're going to pay your invoices as we're not sure this is going to turn out to be what we want. Convert the site to flash and send it us, we'll see whether it's good enough. Thanks."

On Dirt

I met with a client company that needed a logo and a series of brochures. At the meeting, the clients told me they eventually wanted me to create their website as well. Being a newbie, I low-balled the cost for the branding so that I could get the website. After sending a proposal for the site, they told me my quote wasn't in their budget at the time, but that I would definitely get the website work eventually.

Over time, I was asked to do other assignments for their business. They expected me to do it at the same rate that I had initially proposed, to which I agreed. I delivered good designs in a timely fashion, at a dirt cheap rate. They were always happy with my work, which is why they kept coming back to me.

Fast-forward a year later, the client began talking about getting a new website. Per their request, I sent a revised website proposal and was assured by the manager that I would definitely design their website, as they loved my work.

After a few weeks of not hearing from them, I inquired. I was told by the administrative assistant (and daughter of the manager) that she would be designing the website instead.

Moral of the story? You price yourself like dirt, you'll be treated as such.

"I'm not paying for this! Photography is not art—it's just a Xerox of what happened!"

"'Fair Use' means I can use this however I want."

A Different Kind of Betrayal

After mocking up a few designs and sending them to the client, she called me and seemed a bit disturbed and offended.

CLIENT: Yeah, hi. I want to talk about the designs. Why are there naked girls on my website?

ME: Naked girls? Sorry, I have no idea what you're talking about.

CLIENT: Well, I opened the files that you sent me, scrolled down and saw three naked girls kissing. This is incredibly unprofessional; I'm disgusted that you would send me something like this.

[I had already figured what was happening but you can't just say these things straight away.]

ME: All I've sent to you are three screenshots of the design I've made so…

CLIENT: And now I'm seeing a picture of a camel and pictures of a desert. What is all of this?

ME: Ma'am, I don't know how to say this, but what you're seeing are files from your cache. So these are temporary images your computer saves when you go onto a website.

CLIENT: What? Oh, no. That can't be. I've never visited sites like that.

At this point, her husband starts to get involved. I hear him yelling in the background that what I'm saying is "Bullshit! She's fucking lying!"

After a lengthy discussion with a client, I sent them a series of wireframes.

"These do not reflect what we discussed in our meeting in regards to color, look and feel. Too much whitespace. Too sketchy. Too bare. We'll be going with another firm. Thank you for your time."

I responded to the client that these were basic wireframes meant to give her a sense of the structure. I never heard back.

Broken

I once had a client who, while testing his new web site, declared that it seemed to "not be working." He refused to say anything more other than I shouldn't contact him about it. I had no idea what he was talking about, as the site appeared to be working perfectly. I mustered the courage to discuss the situation with a manager at my client's company. The guy went absolutely apeshit on me for "disturbing his peace."

Turns out the company's firewall was blocking parts of the site— something I was unable to diagnose without asking questions (which I was instructed not to do). Either way, it was a small problem that I was able to quickly address.

My client then refused to pay the bill, declaring my work to be subpar...even though they've used the site for several years.

I'm an in-house designer at an event promotions agency. We focus primarily on small bands and small theatre shows—not cool ones, but mostly the friends of my boss. Blue grass, swing, kid's theater, everyone way too old or way too young. We stay in business because we've got two large accounts, but I'd be surprised if the company lasts after those contracts expire.

Anyway, I was responsible for designing a poster for one of these big clients. The poster was for one of their largest shows, which was also one of the largest in the state. I was excited to be given the responsibility as I was still fairly green. I worked late nights and came in twice over the weekend to perfect it with my boss. Finally, after about two weeks of design and a week of edits (way too long, I know), it was ready to go to print. I had Friday off, so I made sure everything was settled on Thursday. When I returned on Monday, I saw the poster. I shit you not: the main title was in Papyrus. Big, huge and glaring Papyrus. Just like Avatar. I asked my boss what happened. He explained that he had to make a few changes to it while I was gone and that he didn't have the correct font on his computer. So he just changed it. He said that he thought it looked better anyway.

At Least It Wasn't By Text

The last time I worked in the corporate world was for a customer loyalty management firm.

I was hired under the guise that I would be a full-time, salaried employee, but found out the hard way that I was actually only hired temporarily to help with designs for their upcoming summer conference.

My first job was to create a "20-page flash animation" that the company could use to impress possible investors. I was given two weeks to complete the task.

When I asked for direction, they told me to "be creative," which was ironic in its abstraction considering it came from a team of micromanagers who seemed to spend their days looking over my shoulder to see if I was doing everything right (not that I knew what "right" was, of course). I was eventually able to convince them to help me with a story board and copy. Never once did I complain, even in light of the 96,000 changes I received from 10 different people along the way.

Over the next three months, I wound up making everything from table tops to name badges—brochures, logos, an entire microsite, updates to the corporate site, and so on.

When the conference was over, I finally broke down and told my 24-year-old supervisor that it was difficult for me to do my work when I was constant being micro-managed.

She let me go the next day via Skype.

"We need you to agree to the legal terms in our contract so that we can sue you easier if your work isn't to our liking."

A friend of a friend contacted me about designing a logo and website for her business. About six days and 30+ different logo versions later, I told her that she really needed to decide on a logo so that we could meet her timeline. She responded, "But you said you'd work with me!"

Fast forward a year. The logo and website were complete, but I was still waiting on payment for several invoices.

After several attempts to contact the client, I gave up and went to work on other projects. When my next big project came to a close, the new client mentioned that my previous client had referred me to her. She'd actually spoken to her recently and was asked to pass on a message to me:

She no longer wanted to move forward with the website because I was "forcing her to be an adult and make decisions."

"We went ahead and copied your signature to a new contract with a few minor modifications, nothing big. Looking forward to working with you!"

- Clients who decreased the project timeline from one month to one week, and cut the price by 40% before signing on my behalf

[*Somehow they were shocked when I said I wouldn't honor the contract, even though I "signed" it.*]

"We need to talk about these alleged invoices."

ME: The project will run you about $800.

CLIENT: Are you being serious or are you joking?

ME: Serious.

CLIENT: Oh… Do you know someone who's as good as you, but cheaper?

CLIENT: Your work has been wonderful, but we have reevaluated our finances and simply can't keep you on. If we have any further work for you in the future, we will absolutely let you know!

ME: I'm sorry to hear that. Yes, please let me know about any future projects.

CLIENT: No problem. If you need to reach us within the next month, just email as we'll be in Hawaii.

"Well, we've paid all the important people. So I guess we could look at your invoices at some point."

"We are calling to inform you that we have decided to go with the other design firm. The board felt your work and studio were too creative."

"If you're going to take my ass to court, you're going to have to come up with something better than you 'programmed it.' That's laughable—the web is littered with site templates for sale, which integrate shopping carts, etc. No rocket science there."